Linen and thread

Creating homewares embellished with embroidery and ribbon

Monique Lyonnet

Linen and thread

Creating homewares embellished with embroidery and ribbon

Photography by Frédéric Lucano

MURDOCH BOOKS

Piping, rick rack, twisted cord, bias tape, looped, embroidered, openwork braid ...
a random inventory of haberdashery terms, a quaint lexicon to be read on the
yellowed label of a cardboard box unearthed in an attic, are these names no
more than nostalgia?

Not at all, all these braids are here, woven in this day and age, and can be
placed on very contemporary linens, accessories and everyday objects.

They decorously underline the edge of a cushion,
elegantly finish the hem of a tablecloth,
subtly conceal an ordinary seam,
cleverly close a bag,
merrily carry an Advent gift...
and above all add a note of fancy to your embroideries.

Monique Lyonnet

comfort

Message cushions

Dimensions
40 x 40 cm and 40 x 50 cm

Materials
45 cm 28 count slate blue
evenweave linen, 140 cm wide
55 cm 28 count zinc grey evenweave
linen, 140 cm wide
45 cm 28 count smoke grey
evenweave linen, 140 cm wide
5.5 m natural linen smooth piping
trim
2 cushions 40 x 40 cm
1 cushion 40 x 50 cm

Embroidery
Chart pages 12–13
1 skein DMC Mouliné stranded
cotton 168, 452 and 932

Stitches used
cross stitch and back stitch using
2 strands Mouliné cotton

Instructions
Cut out one 45 x 45 cm piece, one 35 x 45 cm piece and one 20 x 45 cm
piece in the slate blue linen and the smoke grey linen.
Cut out one 45 x 55 cm piece, one 35 x 55 cm piece and one 20 x 55 cm
piece in the zinc grey linen.
For the front of the cushions, embroider the motifs, centring them in
the largest piece in each colour, then position and sew the piping all
around the edge (p. 135).
Sew a 1-cm double-turned hem along one of the long sides of each of
the two back pieces.
Overlap the hemmed edges of these two pieces of fabric so that you
have either a 45 x 45 cm square for the square cushions, or a 45 x 55
cm rectangle for the rectangular cushion (1 and 2).
Assemble the front and back cushion pieces right sides together, then
sew along the piping so that it will show on the right side.
Turn right-side out.

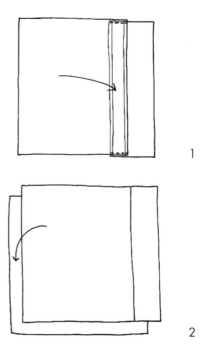

1

2

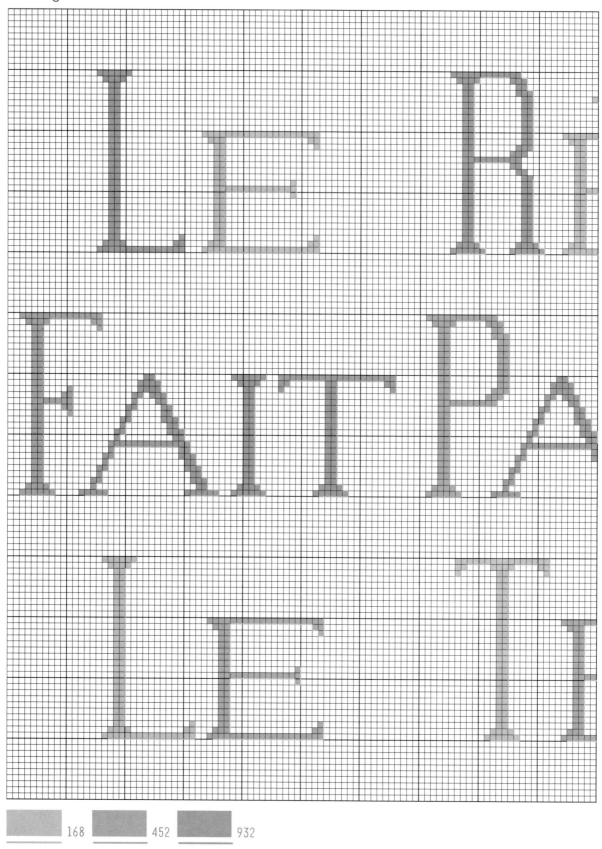

168   452   932

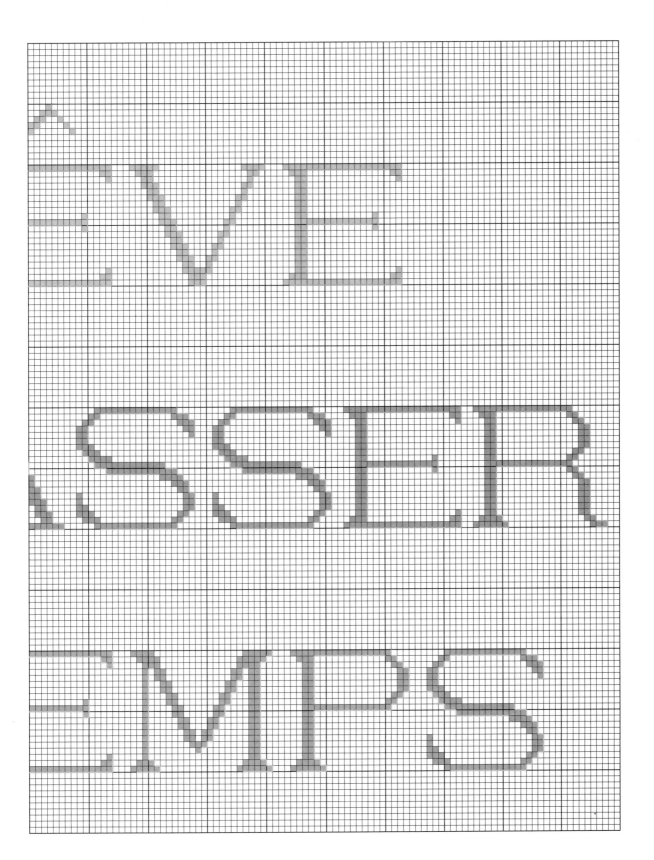

Wording in motif: Dreaming makes time go by

Small 'feather' bolster

Braided throw and pillow case

Small 'feather' bolster

Finished dimensions
11 cm wide x 40 cm long

Materials
40 x 50 cm evenweave linen with
striped white and natural squares
1 m natural linen looped braid
1 bolster 40 cm long and 11 cm wide

Embroidery
Chart pages 18–19
1 skein DMC Mouliné stranded
cotton 642, 644, 645, 647, 648, 3072,
3866 and white

Stitches used
cross stitch using 2 strands Mouliné
cotton

Instructions
Embroider the motifs on the linen, centering them inside the squares.
Sew the looped braid along the two short sides (p. 134).
Topstitch 3 mm inside each edge.
Fold the fabric in two right sides together and sew along the long side
to make a cylinder (1).

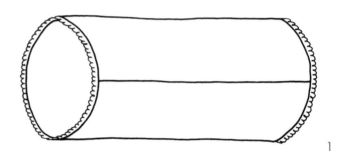

1

Braided throw and pillow case

Dimensions—throw
155 x 155 cm

Dimensions—pillow case
67 x 67 cm

Materials
160 x 160 cm (throw) and 70 x 160 cm (case) coarse cream cotton/linen blend

2.7 m (pillow case) cotton/linen flanged cord trim

6.6 m (throw) and 1.5 m (pillow case) green and red feather stitched braid

3.3 m (throw) and 75 cm (pillow case) red feather stitched braid

3.3 m (throw) and 75 cm (pillow case) green and red 'basque' stitched braid

6.6 m (throw) and 1.5 m (pillow case) green and red 'harlequin' stitched braid

3.3 m (throw) and 75 cm (pillow case) red 'hearts' stitched braid

3.3 m (throw) and 75 cm (pillow case) green and red 'edges' stitched braid

3.3 m (throw) and 75 cm (pillow case) green and red 'middle' stitched braid

Instructions—throw
Baste and sew the embroidered braid down both sides, from one selvedge to the other, placing the first braid 40 cm from the raw edge.

Sew a 3 cm mitred-corner hem with a 2 cm turn-in all around the edge (p. 136).

Instructions—pillowcase
Cut out a 69 cm side square for the front of the pillow, then one 58 x 69 cm rectangle and one 32 x 69 cm rectangle for the back.

Cut the square out of the fabric between the two rectangles, this way the selvedges will avoid the need to hem the edges.

Baste and sew the stitched braid down both sides on the centre of the square piece.

Baste then sew the cord trim all around the edge.

Overlap the selvedges of the two rectangles of fabric so that you obtain a 69 x 69 cm square (p. 10).

Assemble the front and back pieces of the cushion right sides together.

Next sew along the trim line so that it shows on the right side.

Turn right side out.

Placement diagram

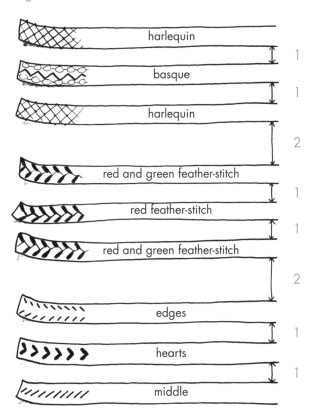

harlequin — 1

basque — 1

harlequin — 2

red and green feather-stitch — 1

red feather-stitch — 1

red and green feather-stitch — 2

edges — 1

hearts — 1

middle

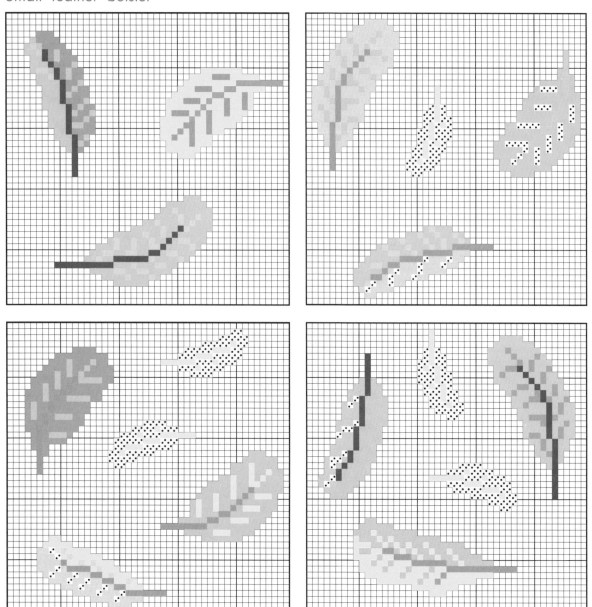

642   644   645   647

648   3072   3866   Blanc

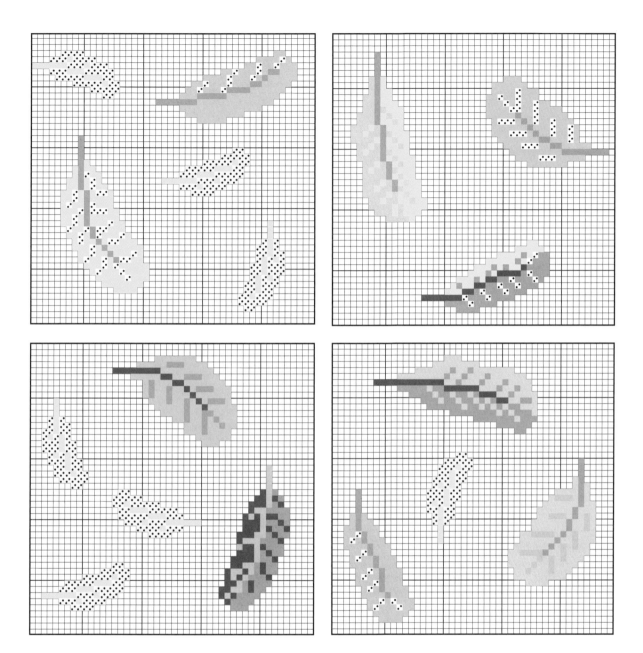

Footstool

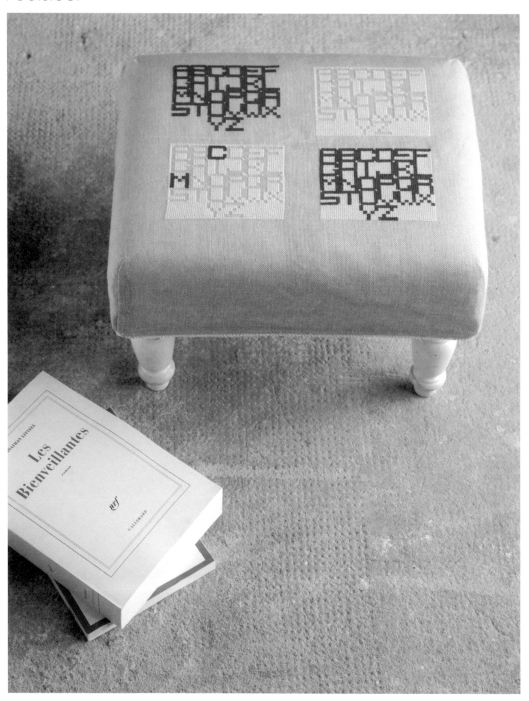

Footstool

Dimensions
30 x 50 cm

Materials
50 x 55 cm 28 count zinc grey
evenweave linen
2.5 m cotton/linen flanged cord trim
1 footrest 30 x 55 cm

Embroidery
Chart pages 24—25
2 skeins DMC Broder Spécial No. 25
cotton 498
2 skeins DMC Broder Spécial No. 25
cotton 822

Stitch used
cross stitch using 1 strand cotton

Instructions
Embroider the motifs on the linen, centring them.
Position the embroidered cloth right side down on the footrest,
    centring it.
Drape the corners (1), pin, then sew them.
Cut off the excess fabric on each corner.
Overlock the edges together.
Sew the cord trim all around the edge (p. 135).
Topstitch 3 mm inside the edge.

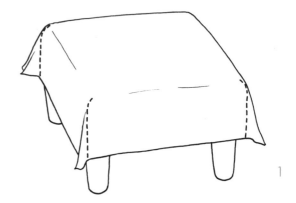

1

Magazine holder and back cushion

Dimensions—magazine holder
50 x 170 cm

Dimensions—cushion
25 x 50 cm

Materials—magazine holder
100 x 180 cm 30 count natural evenweave linen
7 m natural linen webbing, 2 cm wide

Materials—back cushion
55 x 55 cm 30 count natural evenweave linen
1.1 m natural linen twill tape, 2 cm wide
1 cushion 25 x 50 cm

Embroidery
Chart pages 26—27
2 skeins DMC Mouliné stranded cotton 3865

Stitches used
cross stitch using 2 strands Mouliné cotton

Instructions—magazine holder
Cut out one 60 x 180 cm rectangle and two 35 x 48 cm rectangles for the pocket fronts.
Baste the tape so that it encases one of the 48 cm edges on each of the pocket fronts (p. 134).
Turn over a 5 cm hem towards the right side, iron, then sew the encased edge (1).
Embroider the pocket front starting 2.5 cm from the tape.
Baste the tape so that it encases the edges of the large linen rectangle, then baste a 5 cm mitred-corner hem on the right side of the fabric (p. 137).
Slip a pocket front under the hem at each end of the large piece (2).
Sew all around the edge on top of the tape. Remove the basting.

Instructions—cushion
Embroider three diamonds on the linen, centring the motif.
Sew the linen tape to encase the edges of two opposite sides (p. 134).
Fold the fabric in two, right sides together.
Sew the non-encased sides together 1.5 cm inside the edge. Turn right side out.

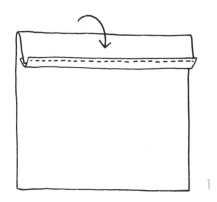

1

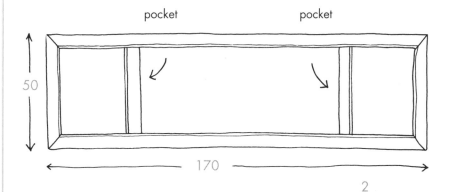

pocket   pocket

50

170

2

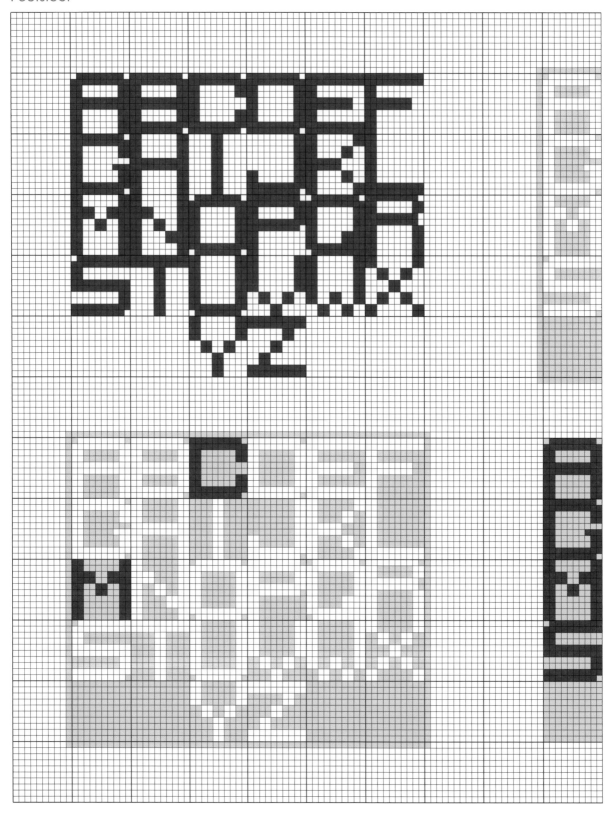

498   822

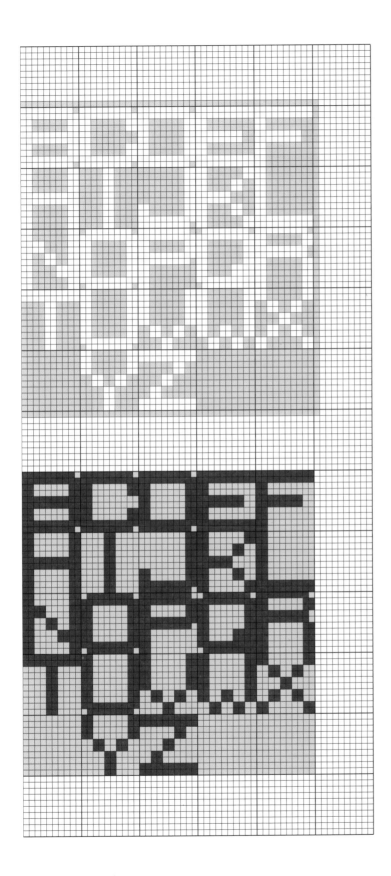

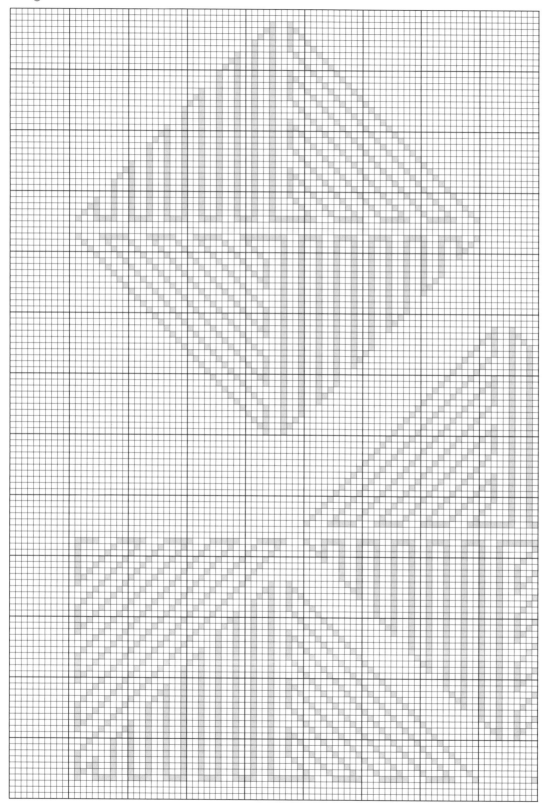

3865

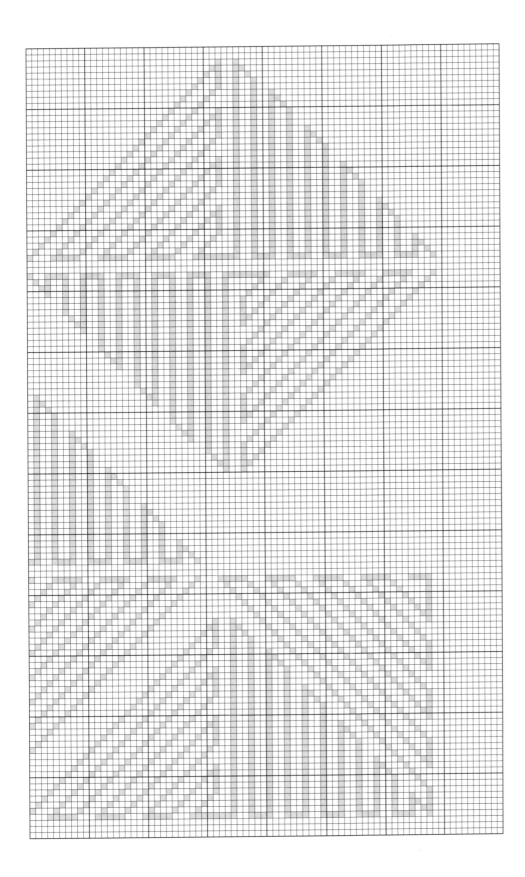

Reversible pockets

'Tiled' hemstitch cushion

Reversible pockets

Dimensions
large pocket: 40 x 40 cm
medium pocket: 30 x 30 cm
small pocket: 20 x 20 cm

Materials—large pocket
45 x 65 cm 30 count natural evenweave linen
45 x 65 cm 30 count ivory evenweave linen
90 cm two-tone linen flanged cord trim
1 large 9 cm nappy pin

Materials—medium pocket
35 x 50 cm 30 count checked evenweave linen
35 x 50 cm 30 count natural evenweave linen
65 cm two-tone linen flanged cord trim
1 steel 7 cm nappy pin

Materials—small pocket
25 x 35 cm linen with white polka dots
25 x 35 cm 30 count natural evenweave linen
50 cm two-tone linen flanged cord trim
1 steel 4.5 cm nappy pin

Embroidery
Chart pages 32–33
1 skein DMC Mouliné stranded cotton 168, 814, 932 and 3865

Stitch used
cross stitch using 2 strands Mouliné cotton

Instructions
Embroider the motifs on the natural evenweave linen: 16 cm inside one of the short sides for the large pocket, 14 cm for the medium pocket and 10 cm for the small pocket.

Baste and sew the cord trim along the short side furthest from the embroidery for the small pocket and on the short side nearest the embroidery for the medium and large pockets (p. 135).

Baste and sew the cord trim along one of the short sides of the non-embroidered pieces (p. 135).

Position the two pieces of each pocket right sides together. Sew 1.5 cm inside the edges, leaving the side with the cord trim open (1).

Turn right side out. Fold over a 20, 16 or 10 cm flap to close the pockets with the pin (2 and 3).

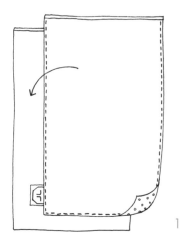

1

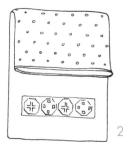

2

3

'Tiled' hemstitch cushion

Dimensions
45 x 45 cm

Materials
45 x 45 cm natural drawn-thread
evenweave linen
45 x 70 cm natural fine linen
2 m natural linen flanged cord trim
1 cushion 45 x 45 cm

Embroidery
Charts and diagrams pages 32–33
2 skeins DMC Broder Spécial No. 25
cotton 822
1 skein DMC Mouliné stranded
cotton 168, 814, 932 and 3865

Stitches used
hemstitch using 1 strand Broder
Spécial cotton and cross stitch
using 2 strands Mouliné cotton.

Instructions
Hemstitch the weave in the square of drawn-thread linen.
Embroider the motifs, centring them inside the middle four squares.
Baste and sew the cord trim all around the front fabric piece (p. 135).
Cut two 35 x 45 cm rectangles out of the fine linen and sew a 1 cm
   double-turned hem on one of the 45 cm sides of each piece.
Overlap the two back pieces to obtain a 45 cm side square (p. 10).
Assemble the front and back pieces of the cushion right sides together
   then sew along the cord trim so that it shows on the right side.
Turn right side out.

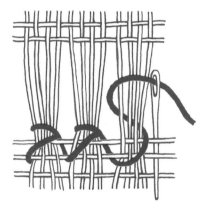

hemstitch

168   814   932   3865

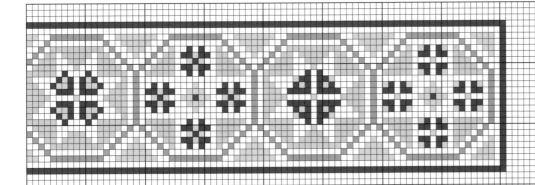

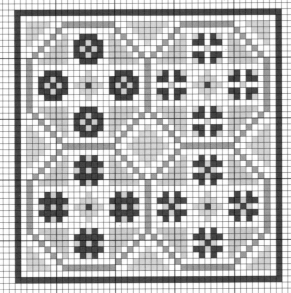

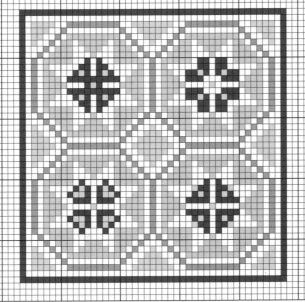

Nappy stacker

Baby comforter

Nappy stacker

Dimensions
20 x 30 x 55 cm

Materials
55 x 140 cm 28 count ice blue evenweave linen
(1 piece 100 x 55 cm and 1 piece 33 x 23 cm for the base, 2 pieces 33 x 10 cm for the yoke)
1.1 m natural linen twill tape 2 cm wide
1 m natural linen twill tape 1 cm wide
70 cm natural linen rick rack
25 cm natural linen cord
20 x 30 cm cardboard
1 x 28 cm wooden angle bar

Embroidery
Chart page 44
2 skeins DMC Mouliné stranded cotton 3865
1 skein DMC Mouliné stranded cotton 498

Stitch used
cross stitch using 2 strands Mouliné cotton

Instructions
Create folds in each side of the rectangle of linen, crease the first fold with an iron 15 cm from each end and topstitch (1).

Cut both lengths of twill tape into two pieces.

Position and sew the 2 cm tape to encase the edge of both 55 cm sides, inserting the two ties halfway up each side (p. 134) (1 and 5).

Embroider the motifs, centring them on each front section.

Mark the other pleats on each side using basting stitches about 10 cm from the top: the first dart 12 cm for the depth, the second 10 cm for the width.

Position the rick rack on the two yoke pieces (p. 135).

Assemble the two pieces right sides together, then sew three of the sides 1.5 cm inside the edge, leaving a 1.5 cm gap in the middle for the hanging loop to pass through (2). Turn right side out.

Turn with right sides together, stitch the base to the upper section (4).

Assemble then sew the yoke onto the upper section that has been narrowed by the pleats (5).

Drill a hole through the middle of the angle bar.

Fold the cord in two, slide the loop through the hole and secure with a knot (3).

Slide the angle bar into the top of the nappy stacker so that you can pull the hanging loop through the opening (5).

Place the cardboard in the base of the stacker.

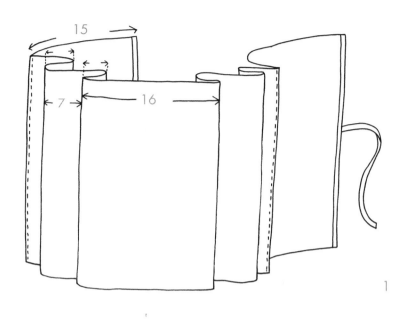

1

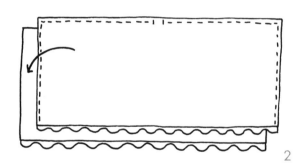

2

3

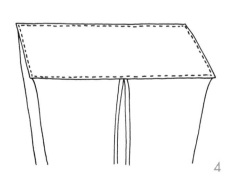

4

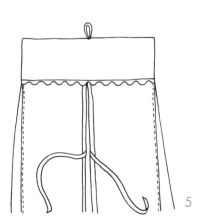

5

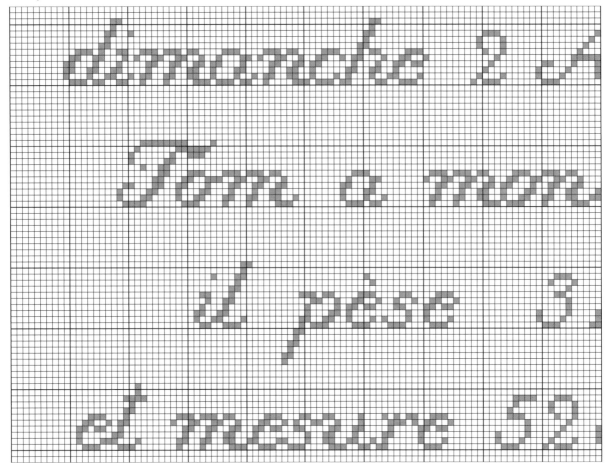

Baby comforter

Dimensions
60 x 80 cm

Materials
65 x 85 cm 16 count natural Aida linen or 30 count evenweave linen
65 x 110 cm natural fine linen for the back
2 m natural linen rick rack
1.8 m natural linen twill tape, 1 cm wide
1 x 100% down child's comforter 60 x 80 cm

Instructions
Embroider the motifs, centring them on the Aida cloth or linen.

Baste and sew the ric rac all around the embroidered piece (p. 135).

Cut one 65 x 77 cm rectangle and one 65 x 33 cm rectangle out of the fine linen.

Cut four 50 cm pieces of twill tape for the ties.

Sew a 1 cm double-turned hem on one of the short sides of each piece, inserting two ties at equal distances from the edges of the larger piece (p. 135).

Overlap the two back pieces to form a wallet closure (1).

Assemble the front and back pieces, right sides together, sewing the other two ties into the seam opposite the first ones (2).

Sew all around 1.5 cm inside the edges so that half of the rick rack extends beyond the seam on the right side. Turn right side out.

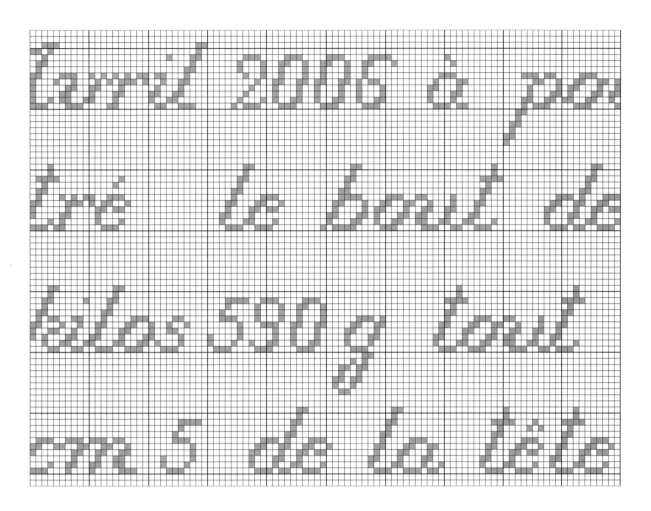

Embroidery
Charts pages 38–40
2 skeins DMC Mouliné stranded
cotton 3865 and 932
1 skein DMC Mouliné stranded
cotton 498

Stitch used
cross stitch using 2 strands
Mouliné cotton

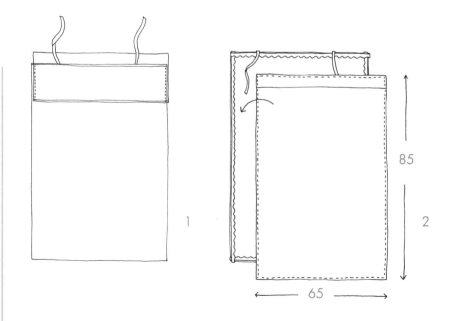

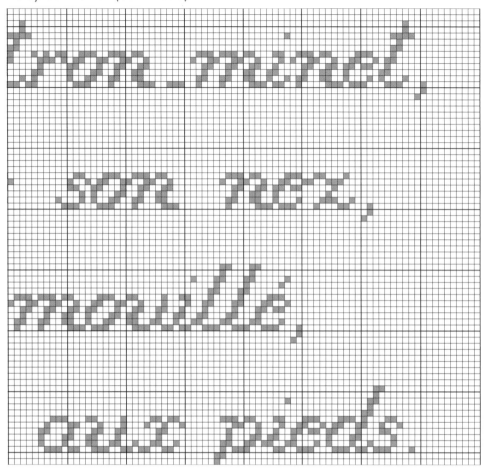

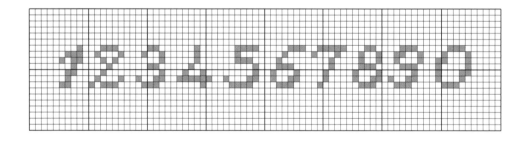

932

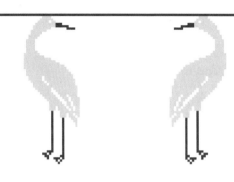

dimanche 2 Avril 2006 à potron-minet,
Tom a montré le bout de son nez,
il pèse 3 kilos 590 g tout mouillé,
et mesure 52 cm 5 de la tête aux pieds.

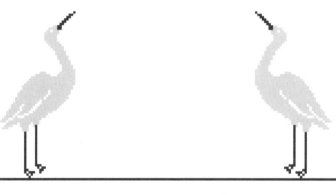

On Sunday 2 April 2006 at break of day
Tom showed the tip of his nose,
He weighs 3 kilos 590g, all wet
And measures 52.5 cm from his head to his toes

Compose your own text by using the alphabet
on page 41 and amending the time of day with
the following phrases...

in the morning
at the end of the morning
at the chime of midday
before afternoon tea-time
after afternoon tea-time
at the end of the day
when night was falling
(very) late at night

Teddy bear's apron

Dimensions
26.5 x 26.5 cm

Materials
30 x 30 cm checked evenweave linen
1 m cotton/linen twill tape
1 cm wide

Embroidery
Chart page 43, alphabet page 41
1 length of DMC Mouliné stranded
cotton 498

Stitch used
cross stitch 1 over 1 using 1 strand
Mouliné cotton

Instructions
Draw the apron on the linen using an erasable fabric marker.
Cut it out, allowing a 1 cm margin.
Cut four 25 cm pieces of twill tape for the ties.
Make a narrow hem with a 0.5 cm turn-in all around the edge, inserting
    a tie at the top and side edges (p. 135).
Embroider the motif on the front, beginning 6 cm from the top of the bib
    section.

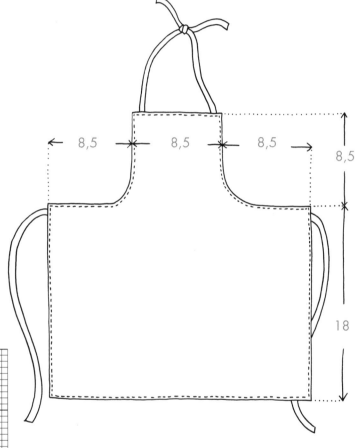

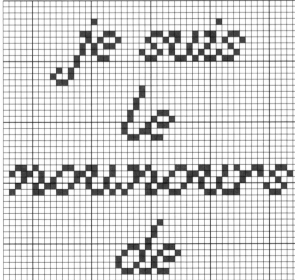

498

Wording in motif: I am the teddy of

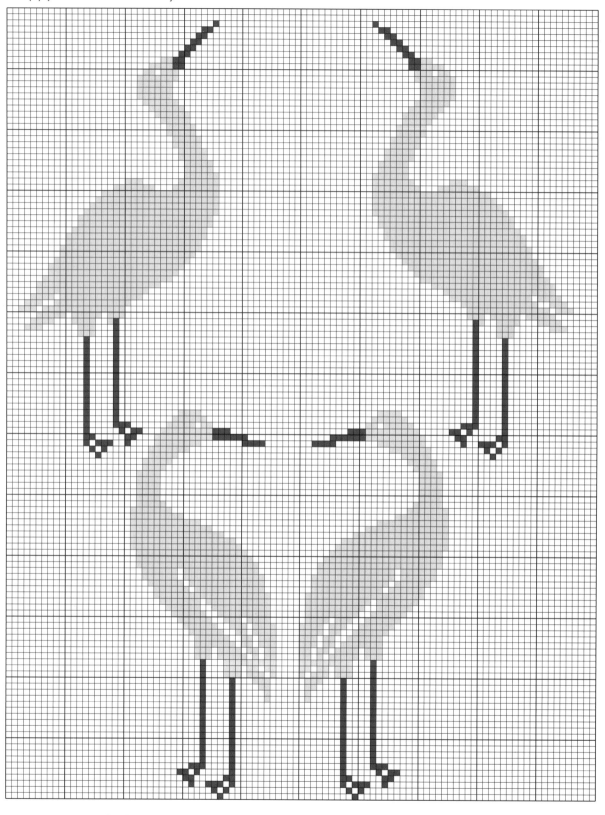

3865   498

Mobile

Baby blanket and checked ribbon

Mobile

Dimensions—mobile
70 cm

Materials—mobile
50 cm blue-and-white checked
linen band, 6 cm wide
50 cm beige-and-white checked
linen band, 6 cm wide
1 natural linen tassel
1.5 m natural linen twisted cord
10 x 40 cm cotton wadding,
3 cm thick

Embroidery
Charts pages 50–51
1 skein DMC Mouliné stranded
cotton 3865 and 3865

Stitch used
cross stitch using 2 strands Mouliné
cotton (p. 51)

Instructions—mobile
Cut six 13 cm pieces of linen band (three blue and three beige check).
  Press a 0.5 cm turn-in at each end then fold in half (1).
Embroider a 'B' in star stitch in the centre of one side of a blue check
  piece; repeat. Embroider an 'E' in star stitch in the centre of one side
  of a beige check piece; repeat.
Embroider the triangle in star stitch, centring the motif along the length
  of the band, the base of the triangle bordering the selvedge.
Use the blue Mouliné cotton on the white squares of the check and the
  white Mouliné cotton on the blue squares.
Proceed in the same fashion for the beige fabric using the beige Mouliné
  cotton.
For the small squares: sew along two of the sides, slip a square of
  wadding inside, then close the last side (1 and 2).
For the small pyramids: sew along two sides, fill the inside with wadding
  (1 and 2), then sew the last side at a perpendicular angle to make the
  pyramid shapes (3).
Thread the twisted cord through each of the pieces with a large wool
  needle, sewing a few stitches each time to hold them in place.
Attach the first piece 6 cm from the end and then space each of the rest
  at 6 cm intervals.
Tie the tassel to the end of the cord.

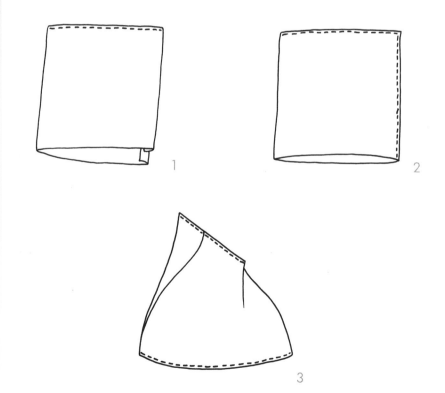

Baby blanket and checked ribbon

Dimensions—blanket
70 x 90 cm

Dimensions—ribbon
5 x 48 cm

Materials—blanket
80 x 100 cm woollen cloth for embroidering with chequerboard weave

Materials—checked ribbon
50 cm blue-and-white checked linen band, 6 cm wide
50 cm natural linen twisted cord

Embroidery
Charts pages 50–51
3 skeins DMC Mouliné stranded cotton 3865 and 3752

Stitch used
cross stitch using 2 strands Mouliné cotton

Instructions—blanket
Sew a 3 cm mitred-corner hem all around the edge with a 2 cm turn-in (p. 136).
Embroider the motifs, centring them inside the woven squares.

Instructions—checked ribbon

Embroider seven diamonds in cross stitch, the first in the middle of the ribbon, the rest spaced at intervals of seven squares of the check pattern.
Cut the twisted cord in two for the ties.
Sew a 0.5 cm double-turned hem at each end of the band, inserting a tie each side (p. 135).

star stitch

Baby blanket

Mobile

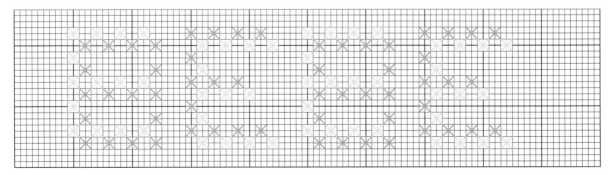

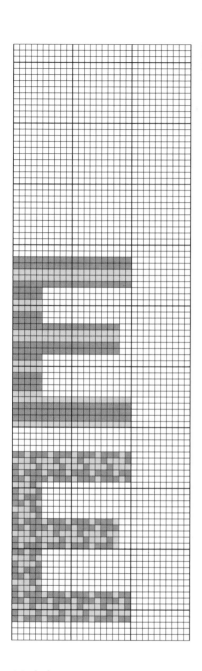

3865   3752   3865 + 3752

Checked ribbon

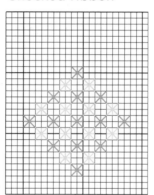

Mobile

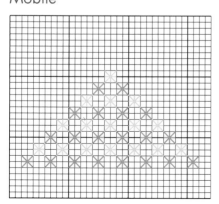

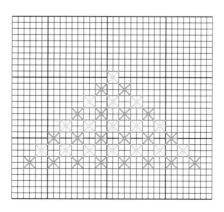

51

share

Two-tone tablecloth

Dimensions

170 x 170 cm

Materials

90 x 180 cm red 30 count
evenweave linen
(2 pieces 90 x 90 cm)
90 x 180 cm ivory 30 count
evenweave linen
(2 pieces 90 x 90 cm)
3.7 m red feather stitched cotton/
linen braid

Embroidery

Charts pages 56–57 and 58–59
4 skeins DMC Mouliné stranded
cotton 498 and 3865

Stitch used

cross stitch using 2 strands
Mouliné cotton

Instructions

Embroider the motifs on each of the squares.
Assemble then sew a red square to an ivory
    square, wrong sides together, placing the
    embroidered sections side by side.
Assemble the two other squares in the same
    way, mirroring the first placement so that
    the four motifs are in the centre.
Press the seams open with an iron then join
    the two sections, wrong sides together.
Press the seams open.
Sew the embroidered braid on top of each
    flattened seam so that it is hidden
    underneath it.
Sew a 4 cm mitred-corner hem all around,
    with a 1 cm turn-in (p. 136).

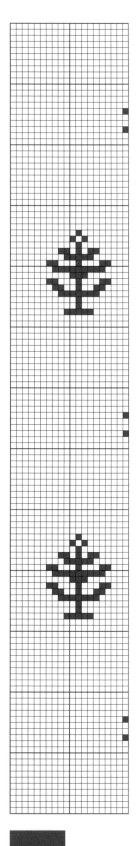

498

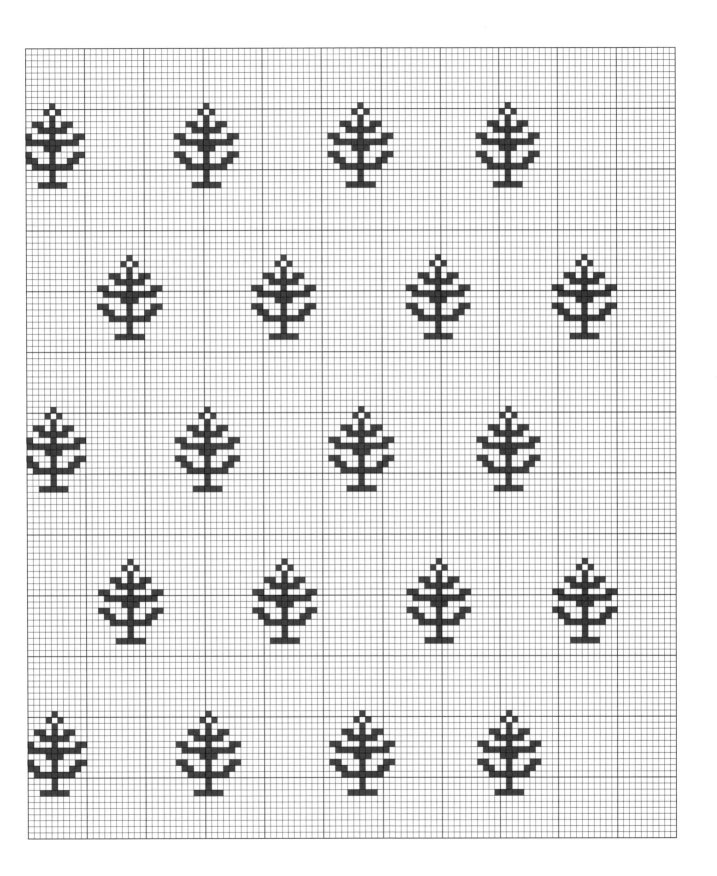

Two-tone tablecloth

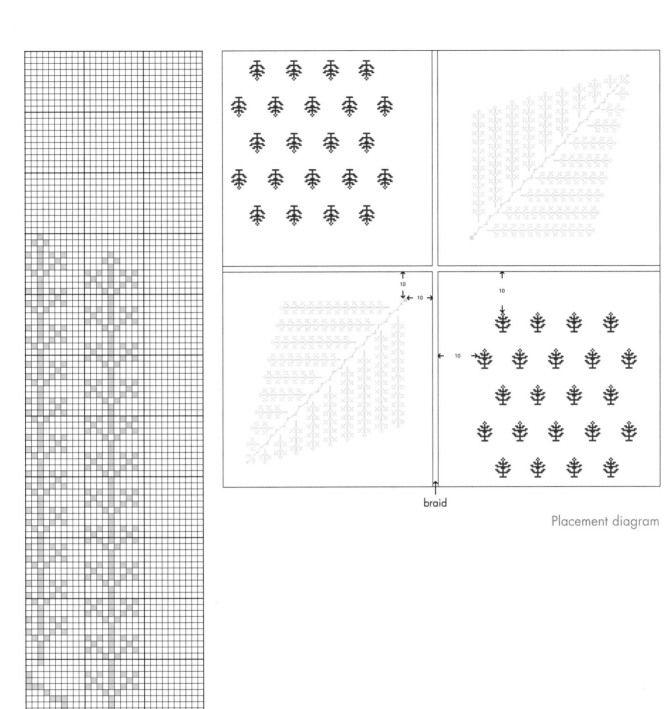

braid

Placement diagram

3865

Advent calendar

Surprise bags

Advent calendar

Dimensions
small pocket: 5.5 x 8 cm
large pocket: 11.5 x 16 cm

Materials
4.6 m red-and-white striped linen band, 5.5 cm wide
35 cm red-and-white striped linen band, 11.5 cm wide
2 m red-and-white embroidered braid, 1 cm wide
24 red and natural wooden mini-clothes pegs

Embroidery
Charts page 64
2 skeins DMC Mouliné stranded cotton 498
1 skein DMC Mouliné stranded cotton 163

Stitch used
cross stitch using 2 strands Mouliné cotton

Instructions
Cut twenty-three 20 cm pieces in the narrower linen banding.
Embroider the number motif on each of them 2.5 cm inside one of the ends (1).
Press the hems at each end and fold into an S-shape to make a pocket at the front and a casing at the back (2).
Stitch to close the casing.
Sew the sides of the pocket.
For the larger pocket, embroider the number motif 6 cm from the end of the linen band.
Make up the large pocket in the same way as the smaller pockets, adapting the measurements.
Slip the braid through the casings.
Fasten the pockets to the braid using the mini clothes pegs.

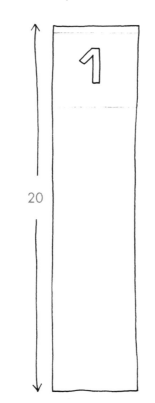

1

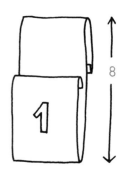

2

Surprise bags

Dimensions

6 x 6 x 17 cm

Materials

20 x 26 cm natural 30 count evenweave linen
30 cm openwork linen braid for the casings
30 cm openwork or looped linen braid
50 cm thin natural linen twill tape

Embroidery

Charts page 65
4 lengths DMC Mouliné stranded cotton 498

Stitch used

cross stitch using 2 strands Mouliné cotton

Instructions

Position and sew the looped braid along one of the long sides of the linen rectangle (p. 134).
Position and sew the openwork braid 4 cm below it (1).
Embroider the motif 3 cm underneath, centring it.
Sew together the two vertical sides, right sides together (2).
Sew up the lower part to close the bottom (3).
Flatten a base 6 x 6 cm, press the folds and sew a seam each side to make 'ears' so that you have a square base (4).
Fold the 'ears' into the square base (5).
Turn right side out. Thread the tape through the stitches of the openwork braid. Tie in a bow.

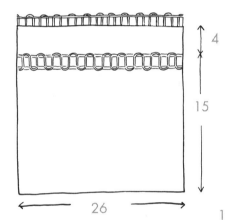

1

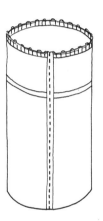

2

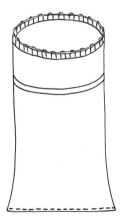

3

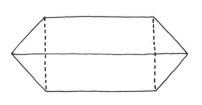

4

5

Advent calendar

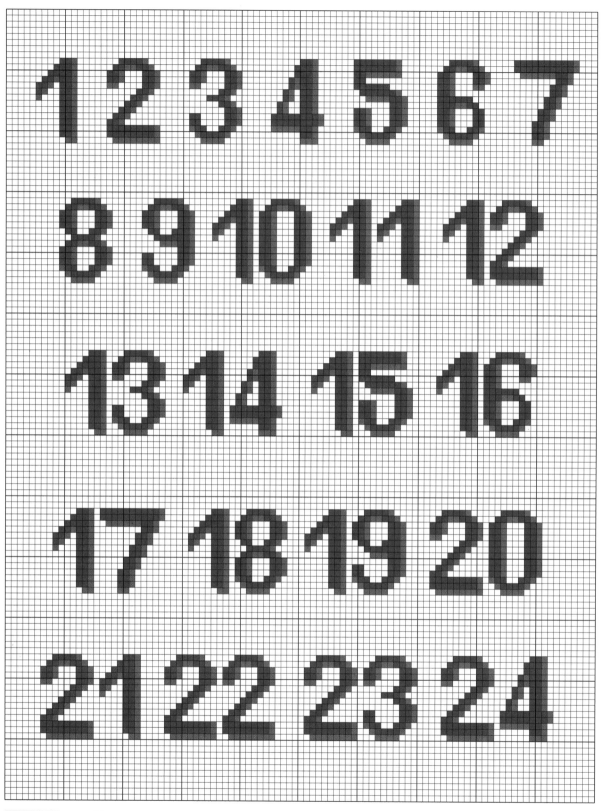

 498 163

Surprise bags

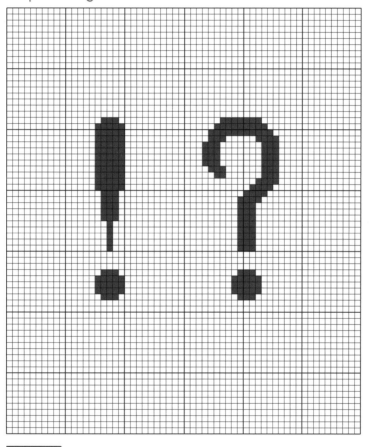

498

Table runner

Napkin rings

Table runner and napkin rings

Dimensions—table runner
50 x 170 cm

Dimensions—napkin rings
5 x 15 cm

Materials—table runner
60 x 180 cm natural 30 count
evenweave linen
5 m natural linen twill tape, 2 cm
wide

Materials—napkin rings
18 cm natural linen banding,
5 cm wide
15 cm natural linen tape

Embroidery
Charts pages 70–71
4 skeins DMC Mouliné stranded
cotton 3865 and 312

Stitch used
cross stitch using 2 strands
Mouliné cotton

Instructions—table runner
Baste the tape to encase the edge all around the linen rectangle
    (p. 134).
Sew a 5 cm mitred-corner hem all around the edge on the right side
    of the work (p. 135). Remove the basting thread.
Embroider the motif above each of the long sides, centring it and
    positioning the lower edge 4 cm above the tape.

Instructions—napkin ring
Embroider the motif on the linen band, centring it.
Cut the tape into two pieces.
Sew a 1 cm double-turned hem at each end of the linen rectangle,
    inserting the ties (p. 135).

Placement diagram

Table runner

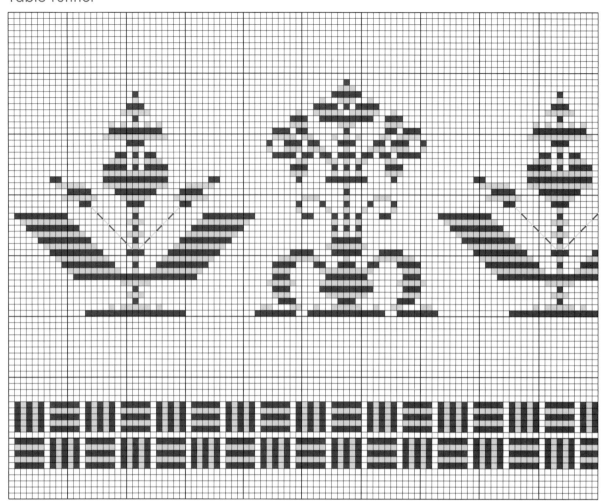

Napkin ring

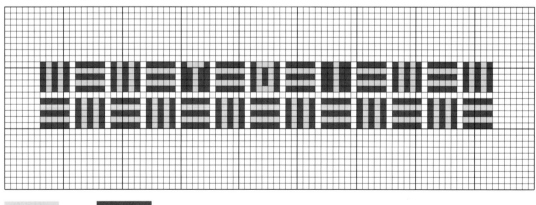

3865   312

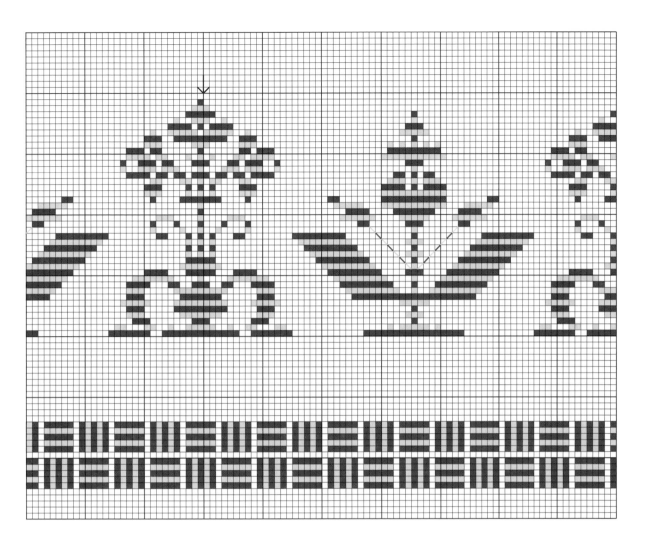

Napkin ring

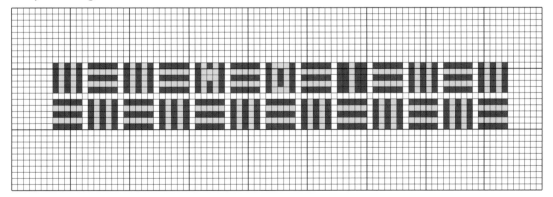

Seagull tablecloth

Dimensions
180 x 180 cm

Materials
180 x 180 cm 30 count natural
evenweave linen
7.3 m natural linen rick rack

Embroidery
Charts pages 76–87
3 skeins DMC Mouliné stranded
cotton 932, 2 skeins DMC Mouliné
stranded cotton white and 931,
1 skein DMC Mouliné stranded
cotton 3853

Stitch used
cross stitch using 2 strands
Mouliné cotton

Instructions
Position and sew the rick rack all around the edge of the linen (p. 135).
Embroider the motif in the centre of the fabric.

Placement diagram

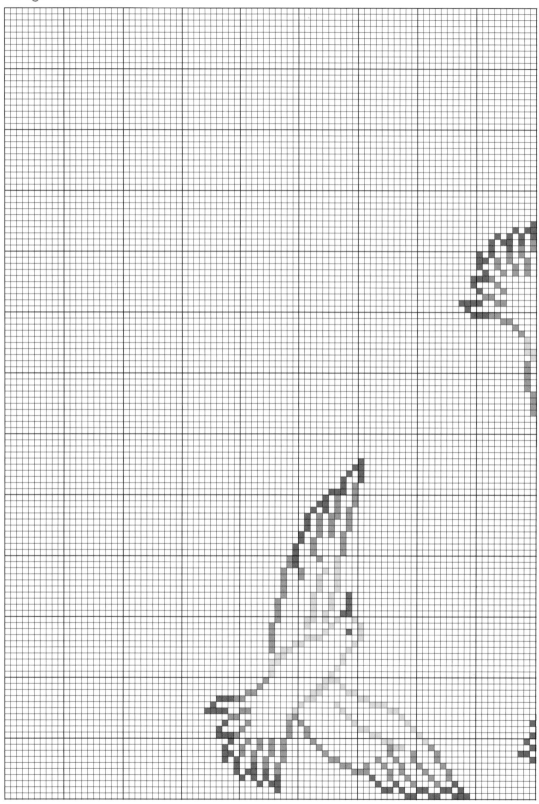

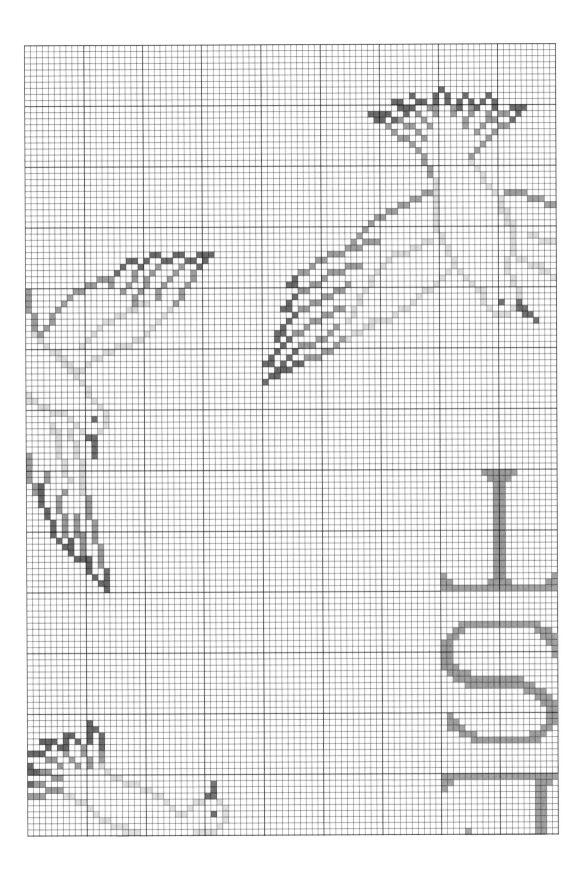

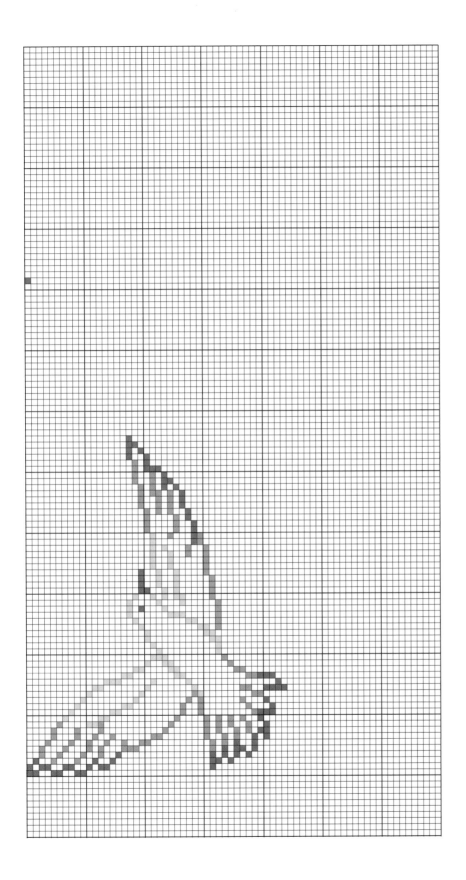

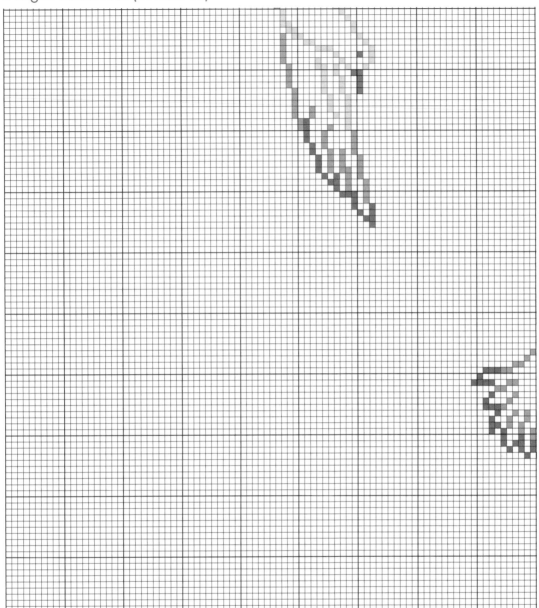

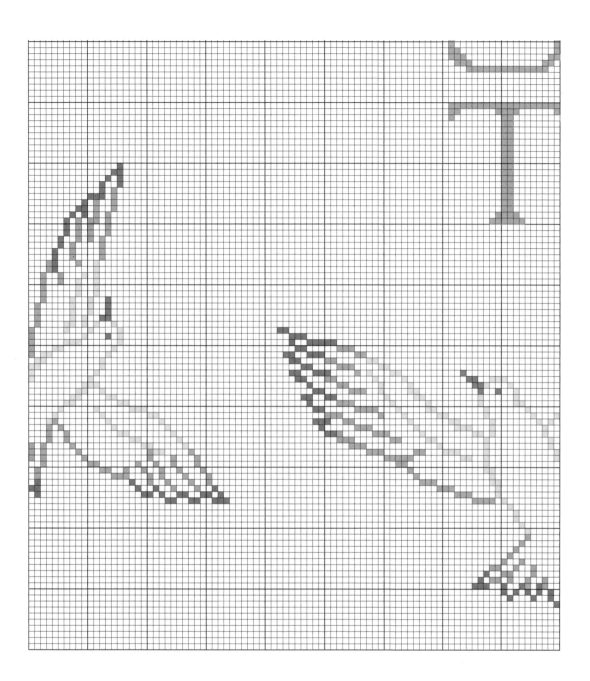

932   931   White   3853

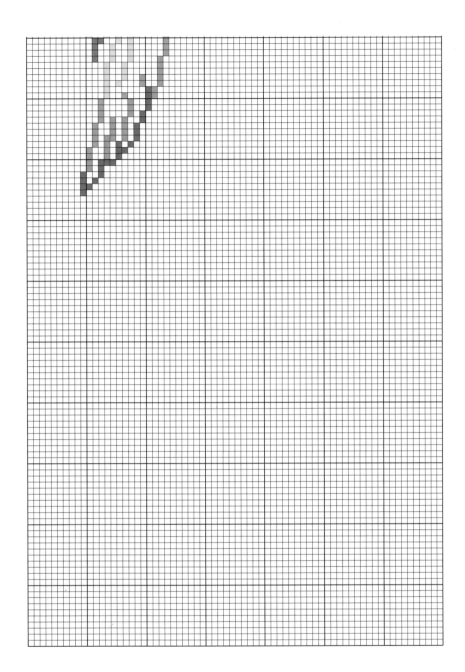

Placemat

Placemat

Dimensions
40 x 50 cm

Materials
50 x 60 cm natural antique linen
2.3 m cotton/linen rick rack with
red stitching

Embroidery
Charts pages 92–93
1 skein DMC Broder Spécial No. 25
cotton 498 and 822

Stitch used
cross stitch using 1 strand cotton

Instructions

Baste the rick rack 10 cm inside the edge of the fabric on all four sides.
Sew a 4 cm mitred-corner hem with a 1 cm turn-in (p. 135).
Sew all the way around on top of the rick-rack.
Remove the basting thread.
Embroider the motifs, leaving a 1.5 cm margin from the horizontal row of
  rick rack and a 3 cm margin from the vertical row.

Linen pots

Dimensions—one pot
14 x 38 cm

Materials
25 x 40 cm plain or polka-dot linen
20 x 40 cm plain or polka-dot linen
12 x 40 cm flexible cardboard

Instructions

Assemble and sew the two linen rectangles along one of their long sides,
  right sides together (1).
Sew together the two vertical sides, right sides together (2).
Sew across the lower edge to close the bottom (3).
Flatten a 10 x 10 cm base, press the folds and sew a seam down each
  side to make 'ears' so that you have a square base (4).
Fold the 'ears' into the square base (5).
Turn right side out.
Fold the fabric inside, slipping the cardboard between the two layers of
  fabric to form a cylinder.
Fold over the cuff (5).

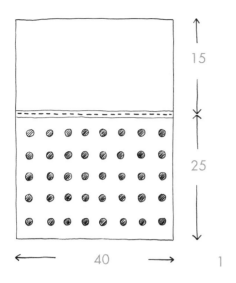

15

25

40

1

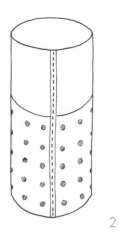

2

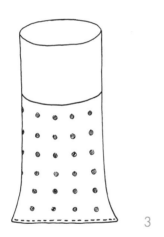

3

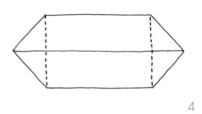

4

5

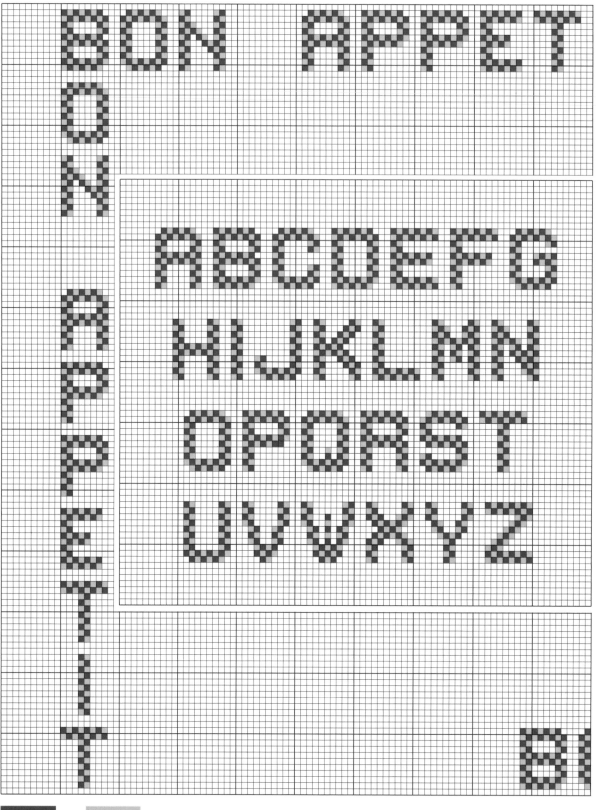

498   822

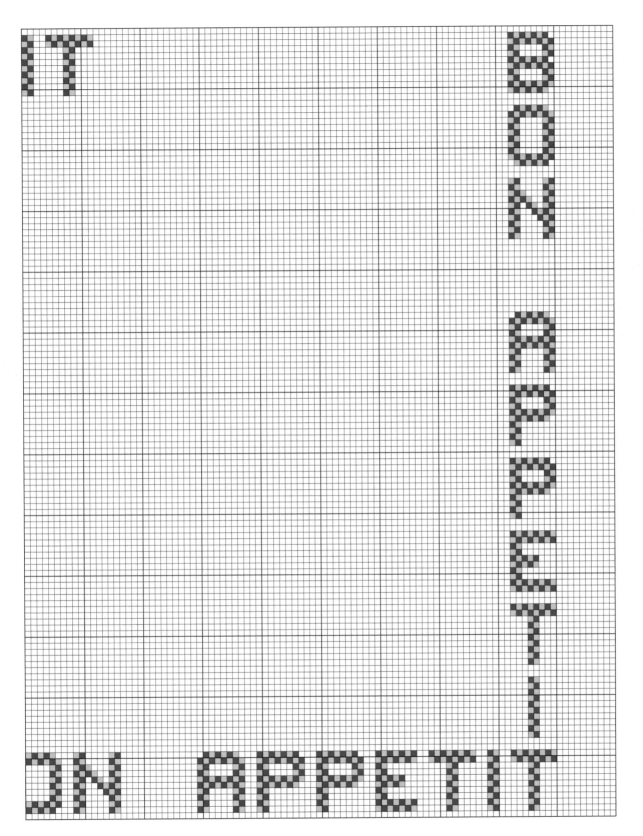

Wording in motif: Enjoy your meal!

Bracelets

Notepads

Dimensions
large pad, folded shut: 21 x 31 cm
small pad, folded shut: 15 x 22 cm

Materials
45 x 115 cm natural 30 count
evenweave linen (large pad)
33 x 85 cm natural 30 count
evenweave linen (small pad)
1 large paper notepad
1 small paper notepad

Embroidery
Chart page 96
1 length DMC Mouliné stranded
cotton 498, 642 and 414

Stitches used
cross stitch, half-cross stitch (tent
stitch) and backstitch using 2
strands Mouliné cotton.

Instructions
Fold the piece of linen in half lengthways.
Embroider the motif 3.5 cm from the fold, centring it vertically.
Sew a 1 cm double-turned hem on each of the short sides (1).
Fold each end of the linen 24 cm towards the centre for the larger model
    and 17 cm for the smaller one, right sides together.
Sew up the sides of the folds (1). Hem the edges between the folds (2).
Turn right side out.

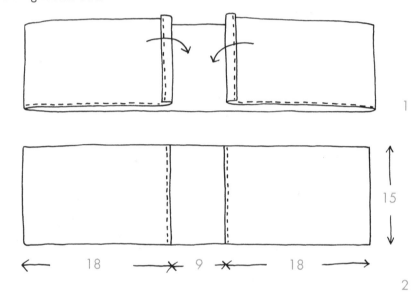

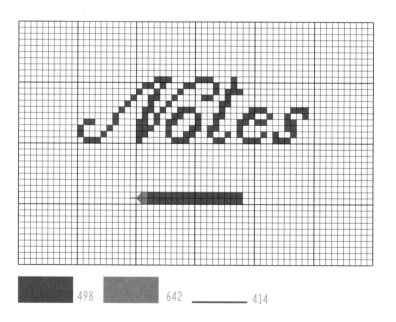

Bracelets

Materials
20 cm natural linen band, 1.5 cm wide
5 cm natural linen twisted cord
3 grey mother-of-pearl embroidery buttons with 5 holes
3 white mother-of-pearl embroidery buttons with 5 holes

Embroidery
3 lengths DMC Mouliné stranded cotton 498 or metallic grey

Stitch used
backstitch using 6 strands cotton

Instructions
Sew a 1 cm double-turned hem at each end of the band, inserting the cord, folded in two, into one of the seams (1).
Sew the buttons onto the bracelet, at regular intervals (2).
The first button should be positioned so that the bracelet can be attached to the wrist.

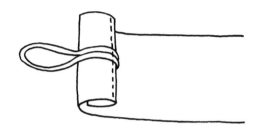

1

2

organise

Pocket tidies

Phone pockets

Pocket tidies

Dimensions
large tidy: 30 x 30 cm
small tidy: 20 x 20 cm

Materials
35 x 70 cm (large tidy) and 25 x
50 cm (small tidy) of 28 count
checked evenweave linen
65 cm (large tidy) and 45 cm (small
tidy) rick rack with red stitching
20 cm (large tidy) and 10 cm (small
tidy) natural linen twisted cord
20 cm (large tidy, and 20 cm (small
tidy) natural linen cord
2 (large tidy) and 1 (small tidy)
steel embroidery buttons with
nine holes
1 wooden angle bar 28 cm long
(large tidy) and 18 cm long (small
tidy)

Embroidery
Chart page 103
1 skein DMC Mouliné stranded
cotton 498 and 3865

Stitches used
cross stitch and backstitch using
2 strands Mouliné cotton

Instructions—large tidy
Cut out one 32 x 32 cm linen square and 2 linen rectangles, one 12 x 32 cm
and the other 22 x 32 cm.
Embroider the motifs 3.5 cm from the top of the small piece and 5 cm
from the top of the medium piece, centring them.
Cut the twisted cord into two pieces, form each into a loop to make the
button loop.
For the small piece: position and sew the rick rack along the long side
beneath the embroidered motif, inserting both ends of both loops (p. 135).
For the medium-sized piece: sew the rick rack along the long side above
the embroidered motif.
Lay the two pieces of fabric one above the other, on top of the square
piece, right sides together (1).
Assemble and sew all around the edge, leaving an opening in the middle
of the top (2). Turn right side out.
Drill a hole through the middle of the angle bar.
Fold the cord in two, slide the loop through the hole in the angle bar and
fix in place with a knot (p. 37).
Sew on the buttons to match the button loops (3).
Slip the angle bar into the top of the pocket tidy so that the hanging
loop passes through the opening.

Instructions—small tidy
Cut out a linen square 22 x 22 cm and two linen rectangles, one 9 x 22 cm
and one 12 x 22 cm.
Proceed as for the large version, embroidering the motif 6 cm from the
top of the medium-sized piece (1-2-4). Insert a single button and sew
on a single button to match.

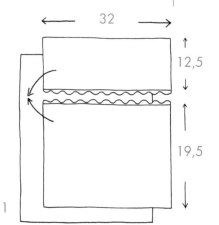

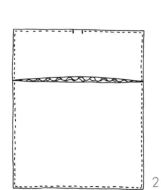

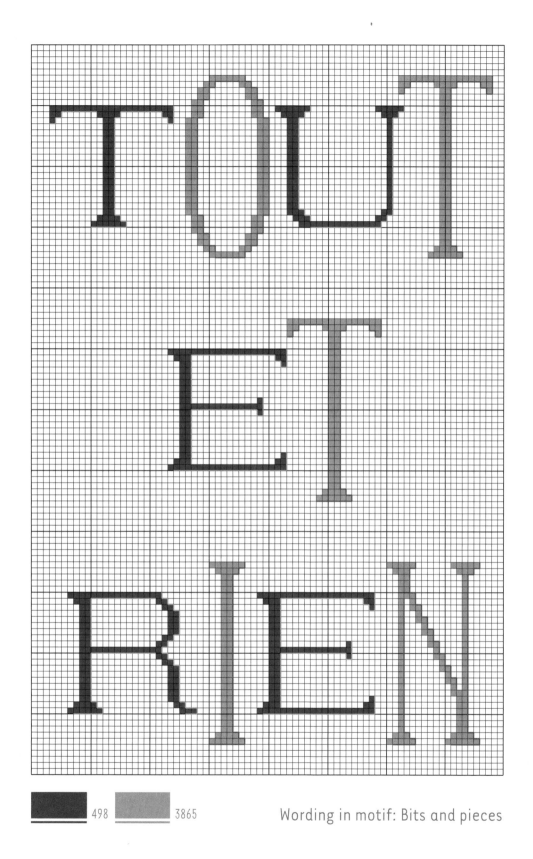

498   3865   Wording in motif: Bits and pieces

Phone pockets

Dimensions
11.5 x 16 cm

Materials
40 cm striped linen band,
11.5 cm wide
15 cm looped linen braid/rick rack
1.3 m natural linen cord

Embroidery
Charts page 105
1 length of DMC Mouliné stranded
cotton 498 or 3865

Stitch used
cross stitch using 2 strands
Mouliné cotton

Instructions
Embroider the motif on the linen band, centring it either on the flap or
the body of the pocket (1).
Position and sew the braid or rick rack on one of the short sides (p. 135).
Hem the other end then fold the fabric over 14 cm, wrong sides together.
Slip the ends of the cord between the two layers of fabric (2).
Close the sides.
Topstitch the material over the ends of the cords (3).

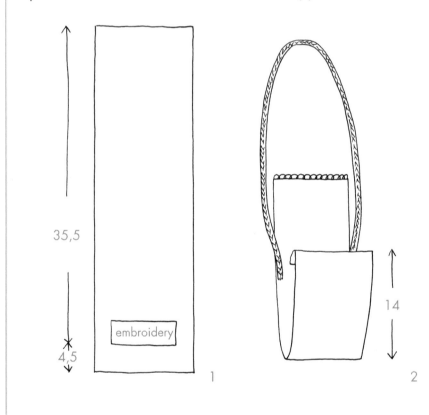

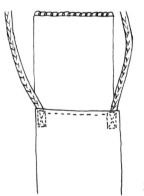

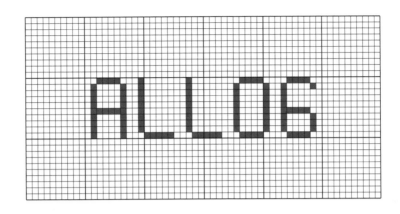

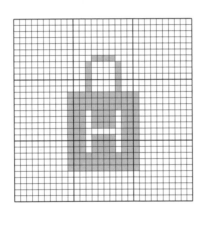

498   3865

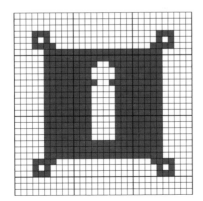

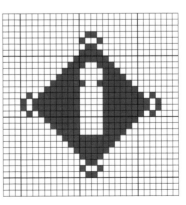

Toiletries bag

Shelf edging

Toiletries bag

Dimensions
28 x 25 cm

Materials
30 x 60 cm natural coated* linen
30 x 30 cm natural 30 count linen
Aida or evenweave cloth
60 cm red rick rack
20 cm natural linen twisted cord
2 steel embroidery buttons with
9 holes

Embroidery
Charts pages 110–111
1 skein DMC Mouliné stranded cotton 3865 and 1 length 498
Stitch used: cross stitch using 2 strands Mouliné cotton

*waterproofed

Instructions
Cut the linen Aida or evenweave cloth in half.
Embroider the motif in the centre of one of the pieces.
Assemble and sew the pieces, right sides together, to each end of the coated linen (1).
Cut the cord in two.
Position and sew the rick rack along the two edges of Aida. On the top one (p. 135), insert the ends of the cords, folded into loops, into the embroidery side of the seam, leaving a 15 cm gap between them (1).
Fold the whole piece in two, right sides together.
Pin, then sew the sides (2).
Flatten a 10 cm base, press the folds and sew a seam on each side to form 'ears' so you have a flat base (3).
Fold the 'ears' into the base. Turn right side out.
Fold over the embroidered flap and sew on the buttons so they are opposite the button loops.

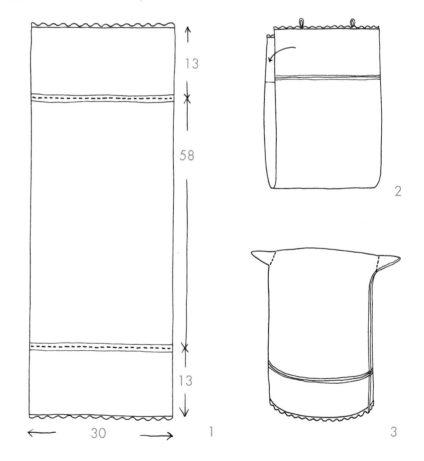

Shelf edging

Dimensions
12 cm high

Materials
1 band of striped 28 count linen,
11.5 cm wide
red or natural linen rick rack

Embroidery
Charts pages 110–111
1 skein DMC Mouliné stranded
cotton 3865 and 498

Stitch used
cross stitch using 2 strands
Mouliné cotton

Instructions
Embroider the motifs 3 cm from the bottom of the band, centring them
along the length.
Position the rick rack under the bottom selvedge, with half showing
(1 and 2).
Sew a 1 cm double-turned hem at each end.

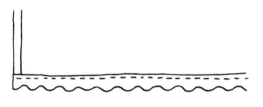

1

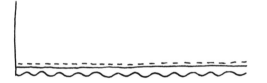

2

Toiletries bag

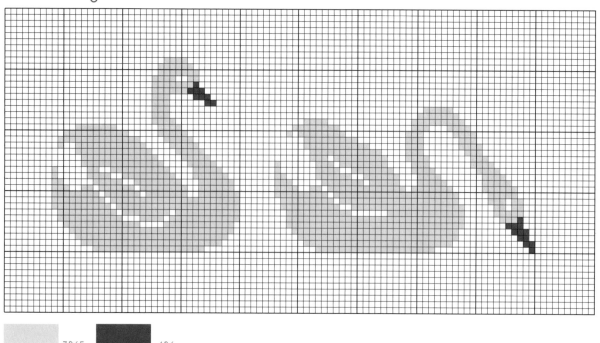

3865   496

Shelf edging

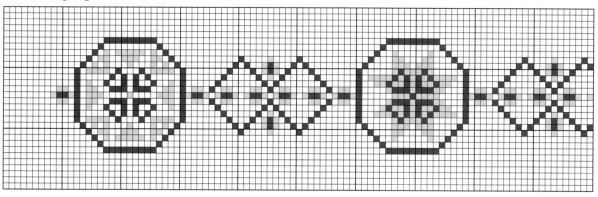

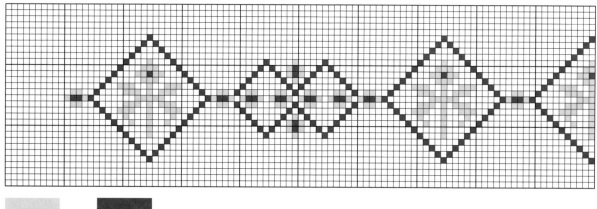

3865   496

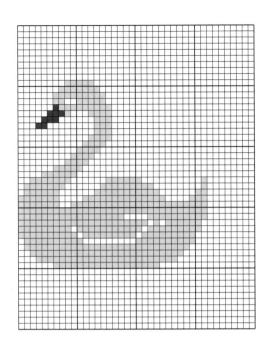

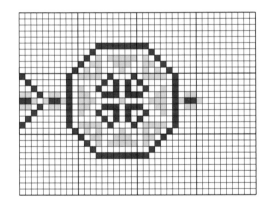

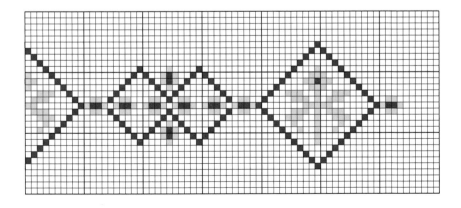

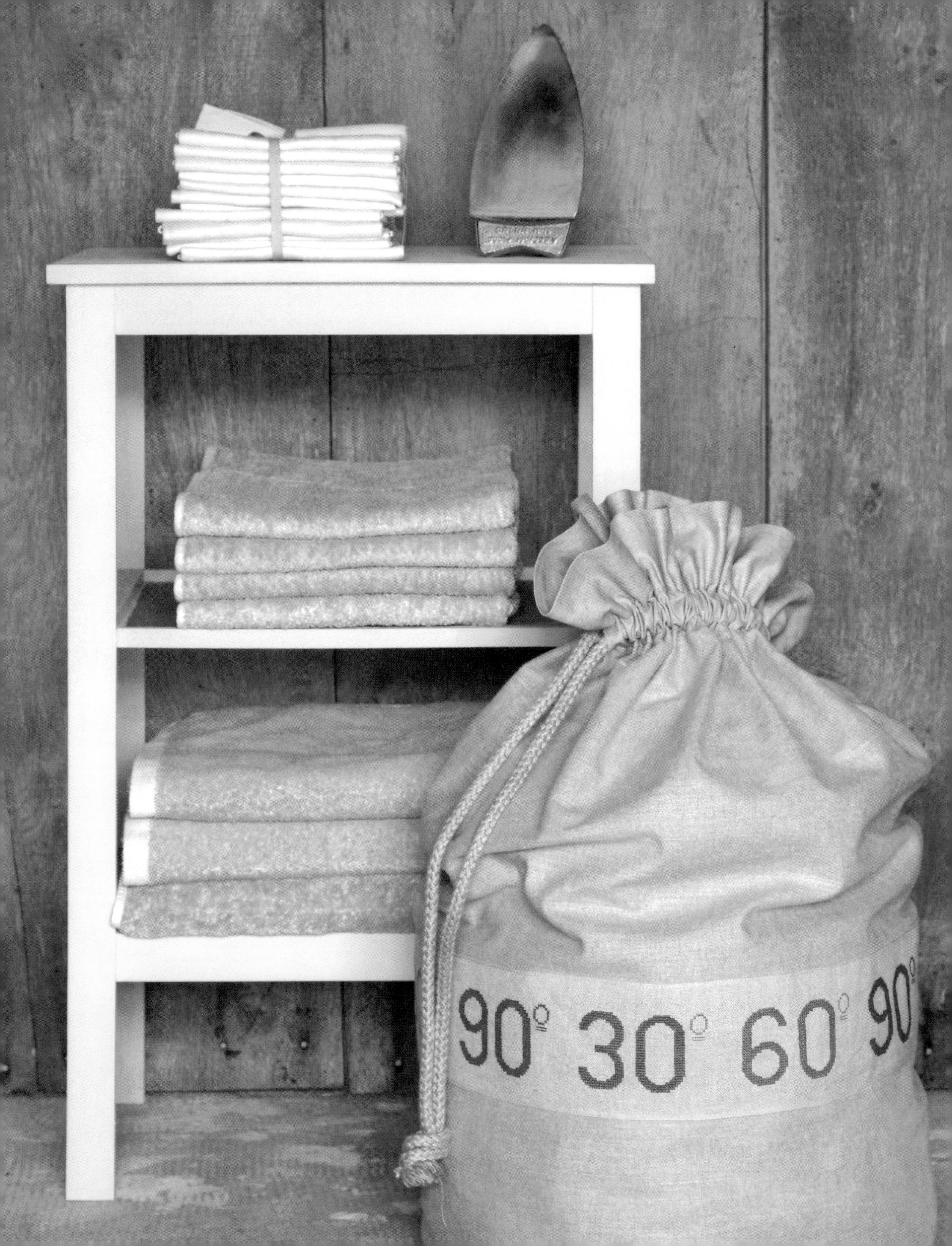
90° 30° 60° 90°

Laundry bag

Dimensions
30 x 30 x 75 cm

Materials
100 x 120 cm natural coated linen
1.2 m 28 count natural band,
10 cm wide
3.2 m thick natural linen cord

Embroidery
Chart pages 114–115
1 skein DMC Mouliné stranded
cotton 158, 333 and 498

Stitches used
cross stitch and backstitch using
2 strands Mouliné cotton

Instructions
Embroider the motifs along the centre of the band.
Position and sew the band on the non-coated side of the linen (1).
At the top, on the right side, turn over a 12 cm hem and secure it with
two parallel rows of stitching 4 cm apart to make the drawstring
casing (2).
Pin and sew the vertical sides together, right sides together (3).
Sew the lower edge to close the bottom (4).
Flatten a 30 cm base, press the folds and sew a seam on each side to
make 'ears' so that you have a square base.
Fold the 'ears' into the square base (5). Turn right side out.
Using scissors, make a slit in the casing on each side of the bag so that
the drawstring can be threaded through.
Cut the cord in two. Using a large safety pin, slide one of the pieces of
cord into one of the slits and thread it all the way around the bag,
pulling it out through the same slit and tie the two ends of the cord
together. Repeat the process with the other piece of cord, inserting it
into and pulling it out of the opposite slit.

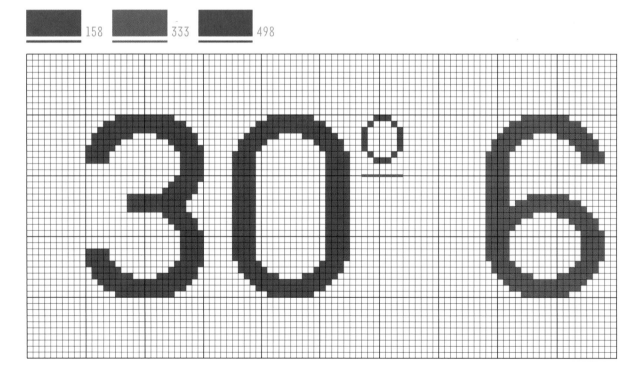

158   333   498

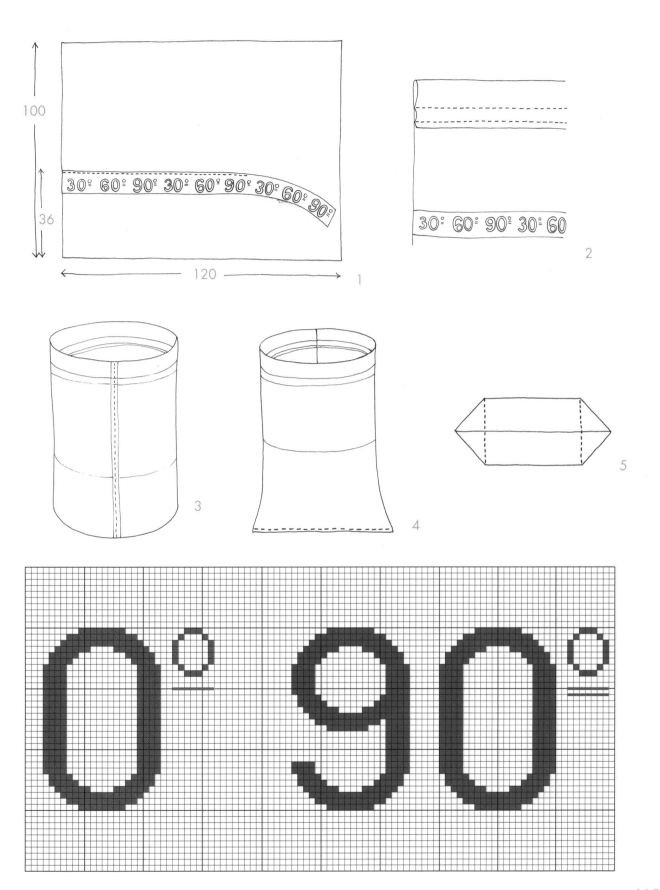

Window bag

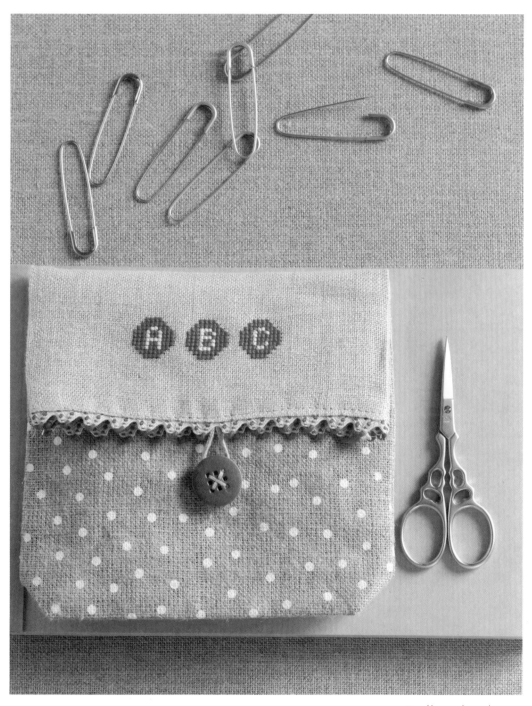

Polka-dot bag

Window bag

Dimensions
15 x 19 x 30 cm

Materials
35 x 90 cm linen with a large polka dot pattern
20 x 20 cm 30 count natural evenweave linen
1.5 m red rick rack
1.2 m thick linen cord

Embroidery
Chart page 120
1 skein DMC Mouliné stranded cotton 498, 2 lengths of DMC Mouliné stranded cotton 3865

Stitch used
cross stitch using 2 strands Mouliné cotton

Instructions
Embroider the motifs in the centre of the square of linen.

Cut out one 35 x 77 cm piece and two 6.5 x 35 cm pieces in the polka-dot linen for the cuff.

Draw a 15 cm square using a fabric marker on the wrong side of the large piece, 11 cm from the top and centred horizontally.

Snip into the centre of this square using scissors and cut 1 cm inside the lines. Notch the corners on the diagonal.

Fold back and baste the edges towards the wrong side (1).

Cut four 17 cm pieces of red rick rack, baste them around the window, on the wrong side, with half of the rick rack showing on the right side (2).

Position and baste the square of linen, taking care to centre it properly in the window (3). Sew two rows of stitches around the window, on the right side, 5 mm apart. Remove the basting thread.

Position and sew the rick rack on one of the long sides of each cuff piece (p.135), treating the reverse of the polka-dot fabric as the right side.

Assemble and sew the cuff pieces, right against wrong side along the two short sides of the large piece, leaving two openings 12 cm apart (4).

Cut the cord in two, slip the ends into the openings and attach with a few stitches.

Fold the piece in two, right sides together, and sew up the sides (5).

Fold the cuffs to the outside and topstitch around the edge just above the rick rack.

Flatten a 15 cm base, press the folds and sew a seam on each side to make 'ears' so that you create a flat base (6). Cut the 'ears' 1 cm from the seam and overlock the edges together. Turn right side out.

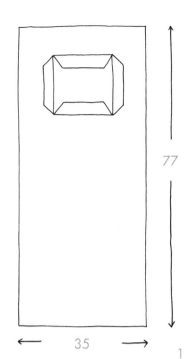

77

35

1

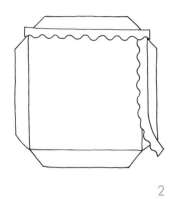

2

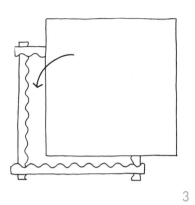

3

4

5

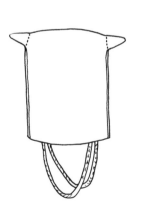

6

Window bag Alphabet

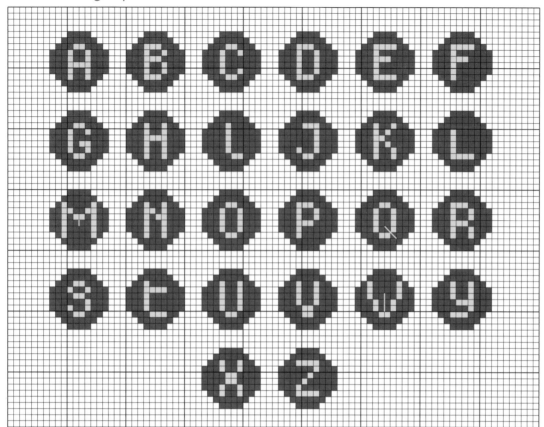

Window bag

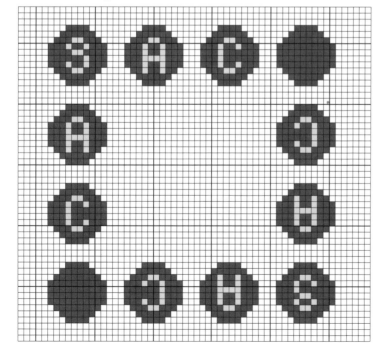

498   3865

Polka-dot pocket

Dimensions
3 x 14 x 14 cm

Materials
17 x 32 cm linen with a small white polka-dot pattern
2 pieces of natural 30 count even-weave linen, each 10 x 17 cm
35 cm rick rack with red stitching
10 cm natural linen twisted cord
1 steel embroidery button with 9 holes

Embroidery
Chart page 121
2 lengths of DMC Mouliné stranded cotton 498 and 1 length 3865

Stitch used
cross stitch using 2 strands Mouliné cotton

Instructions
Embroider the motif on one of the plain pieces of linen, centring it.

Position and sew the rick rack along one of the long sides of each of the plain linen pieces, inserting the cord folded in two in the centre of the embroidered piece to make the button loop.

Assemble and sew these pieces right sides together to the short sides of the polka-dot linen (1). Fold the resulting piece in two, right sides together, and sew up the sides (2).

Flatten a 3 cm base, press the folds and sew a seam down each side to make 'ears' so that you have a flat base (3).

Fold the 'ears' into the base. Turn right side out.

Sew on the button opposite the button loop.

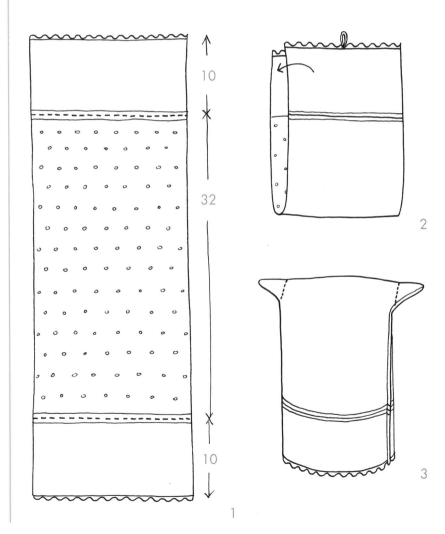

Apron and tea towels

Apron and tea towels

Dimensions—apron
105 x 100 cm

Dimensions—single tea towel
47 x 72 cm

Materials—apron
110 cm x 110 cm ivory antique linen
50 x 50 cm 30 count checked even-weave linen
85 cm cotton/linen flanged cord trim
2.6 m cotton/linen twill tape, 2 cm wide

Materials—single tea towel
50 x 75 cm 30 count checked even-weave linen
20 cm cotton/linen twill tape

Embroidery
Chart pages 126–127
1 skein DMC Mouliné stranded cotton 312, 498 and 642

Stitch used
cross stitch using 2 strands Mouliné cotton

Instructions—apron
Draw the outline of the apron using a fabric marker on the piece of antique linen, positioning the top of the bib on one of the selvedges of the fabric.
Cut out the rounded sections of the bib, leaving a 1.5 cm margin (1).
Cut two pieces of flanged cord trim, one 35 cm and one 50 cm.
Position and sew the small piece of cord trim along the top of the bib (p. 135) and fold over a 4 cm hem towards the right side (2).
Cut 60 cm of twill tape to go around the neck and two 1 m pieces to go around the waist.
Position and firmly sew the smaller piece of tape to each side of the bib (3).
Sew a 1 cm double-turned hem around the rounded sections and the bottom of the apron. Insert a piece of tape into the hem at a right angle at waist level, and stitch firmly (p. 135).
Position and sew the rest of the cord trim onto one edge of the piece of check linen (p. 135). Fold over a 4 cm hem towards the right side of the fabric, keeping the squares aligned (4).
Embroider the motifs on the evenweave linen, centering them inside the checks.
Press under and baste a 3 cm mitred-corner hem with no turn-in on the three remaining sides.
Position the pocket in the middle of the apron at the desired height and topstitch around it on three sides 2 cm inside the edge (4).

Assembly—tea towel
Cut the length of tape in two. Sew a 0.5 cm double-turned hem all around the piece of fabric, inserting the ends of one piece of tape in the middle of the long side, and the other in the middle of the short side to serve as hanging loops for the tea towels.
Embroider the motifs, centring them inside the checks of the linen.

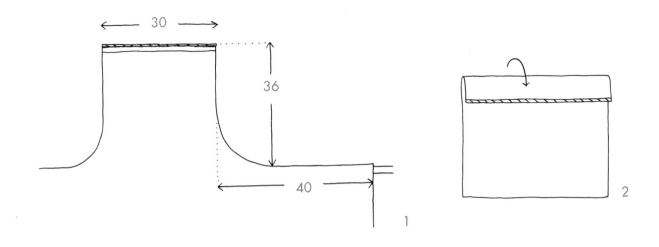

1

2

3

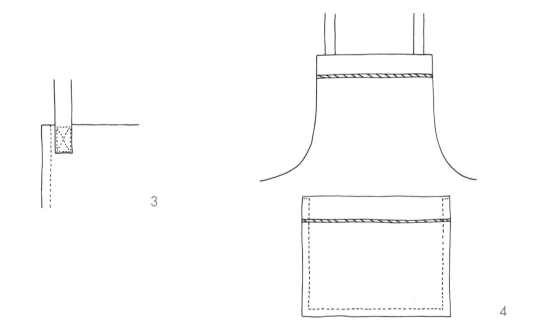

4

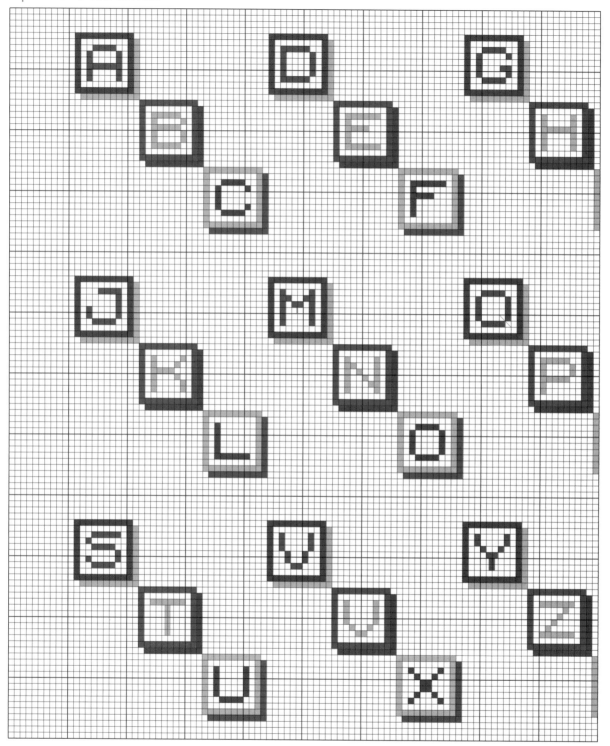

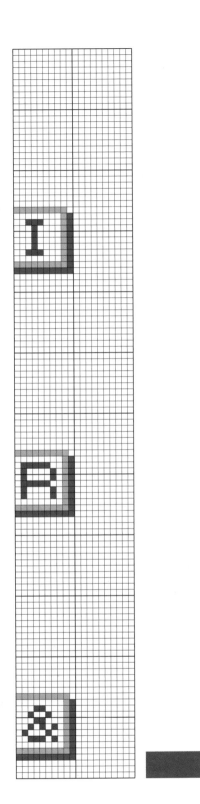

312　　498　　642

Napkin-holders

Little pockets

Napkin-holders

Dimensions
12 x 26 cm

Materials
30 x 35 cm antique natural or
ivory linen
30 cm embroidered linen braid or
rick rack
6 white or steel embroidery
buttons with 9 holes

Embroidery
3 lengths of DMC Mouliné
stranded cotton 398

Stitch used
Backstitch using 6 strands cotton

Instructions—napkin-holder with rick rack

Position and sew the rick rack on one of the short sides of the linen
(p. 135).

Sew a 1 cm double-turned hem along the other short side.

Turn up an 11 cm fold, right sides together.

Sew up the sides.

Turn right side out.

Hem the raw edges along the sides of the flap (1).

Sew the embroidery buttons onto the flap.

Baste a 1 cm hem on one of the short sides of the linen, on the
right side.

Position and sew the braid over this hem to hide it.

Remove the basting.

Continue as for the napkin-holder with rick rack (1).

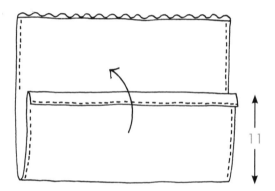

1

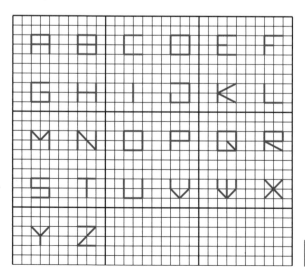

498

Little pockets

Dimensions
16 x 11 cm

Materials
30 cm ivory linen banding,
16 cm wide
20 embroidered linen braid or
rick rack

Embroidery
2 lengths of DMC Mouliné stranded
cotton 498, 642 and 1 length 3865

Stitch used
Cross stitch using 2 strands
Mouliné cotton

Instructions
Position and sew the braid 1 cm from the edge of one of the short sides
   (p. 135).
Sew a 1 cm double-turned hem, sewing along the braid (1).
Sew a 1 cm double-turned hem along the other short side.
Fold up an 11 cm hem to the inside and sew up the sides along the
   selvedges (2).
Fold over an 8 cm flap and press with an iron.
Embroider the motif in the centre of the front flap.

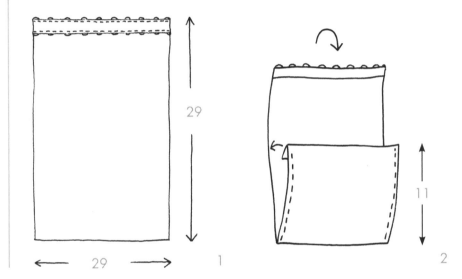

498   642   3865

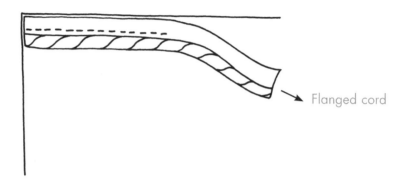

Flanged cord

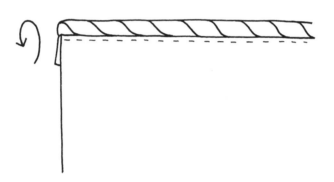

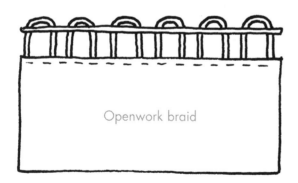

Openwork braid

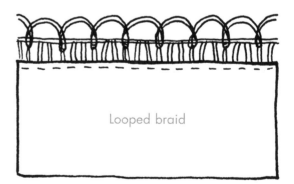

Looped braid

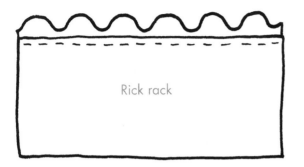

Rick rack

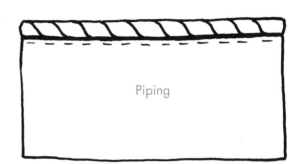

Piping

Tie inserted into hem

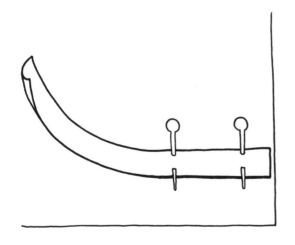

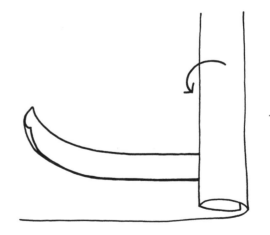

MITRED-CORNER HEM

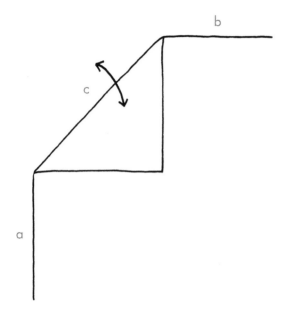

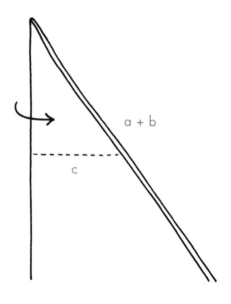

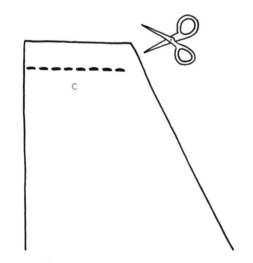

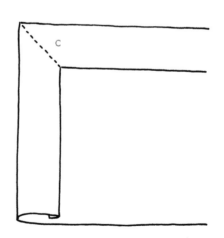

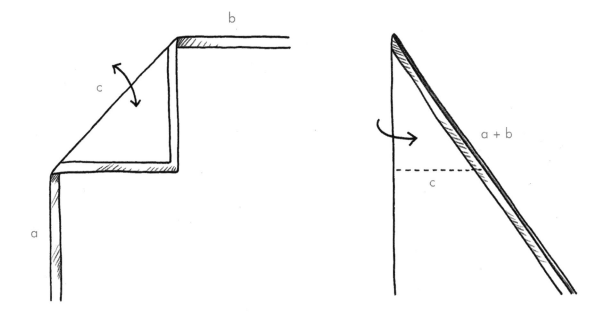

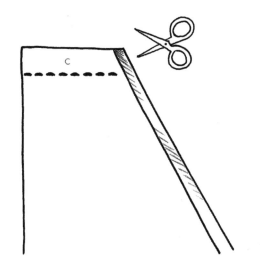

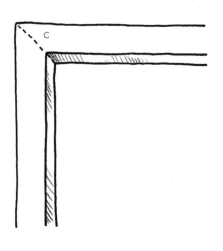

The haberdasher's vocabulary

AIDA CLOTH

A fabric with a small-square weave providing an easier visual guide for embroidering cross stitch.

ASSEMBLE OR CONSTRUCT

Sew together several pieces of fabric.

BASTE

Assemble pieces of fabric temporarily using a large sewing stitch.

BIAS BIND

Enclosing the edge of a piece of fabric with a piece of bias-cut tape or braid.

BIB

The part of an apron that covers the chest.

CASING OR CHANNEL

Fold of fabric through which a drawstring is passed.

CORD

Round braid

COTTON/LINEN BLEND

Fabric made with a cotton warp and a linen weft.

CUFF

Section of fabric folded towards the right side.

CUT

Piece of fabric cut according to the dimensions provided.

CUT ON THE BIAS

Cut fabric on the diagonal, at 45° to the grain.

DART

Fold made in fabric to reduce size while keeping fullness.

DRAPE

Wrap fabric around an object to be covered so its shape can be marked.

EDGE TO EDGE

Positioning two pieces of fabric so that their edges are exactly abutted.

EVENWEAVE

Loosely-woven fabric whose perpendicular warp and weft threads allows them to be counted.

FLANGED CORD

Cord with attached flat flange for stitching into seam.

FLATTEN A SEAM

Ironing a seam to make it less bulky.

HANGING LOOP

Piece of braid used for hanging up a tea towel.

LENGTH

Cut length of embroidering or sewing thread.

LOOPED BRAID

Braid with loops along one of the edges.

MITRED-CORNER HEM

Hem corners worked at an angle by cutting away part of the fabric so that they are flatter.

OPENWORK BRAID
Loosely-woven braid similar to openwork stitches.

OVERLOCK
Sewing over the cut edge of the fabric to prevent fraying.

PIECE
Piece of cut fabric ready to be assembled.

PIPING TRIM
Trim with a flat flange and a covered cord edge, where only the cord shows beyond the seam.

PRESS A CREASE
Create a crease in fabric using an iron.

PRESS SEAM OPEN
Ironing a seam along the middle on the reverse side to separate the two fabric edges and press flat.

RICK RACK
Tape woven in a wave-like shape.

RIGHT SIDES TOGETHER
Placing two pieces of fabric together face-to-face in order to sew them on the wrong side and afterwards turn right side out.

SELVEDGE
Woven edge along a roll of fabric's width.

STRAIGHT-GRAIN
Using the fabric in exactly the same direction as the weave.

TIE
Braid for tying to form a closure.

TOPSTITCHING
Visible stitching that holds together a fabric fold.

TURN OVER, UP OR DOWN
To fold over.

TURN-IN OR DOUBLE TURN
The part of the fabric folded into the hem.

TWILL TAPE
Flat braid whose diagonal weave forms a herringbone pattern that enhances flexibility.

TWISTED CORD
Small round braid.

WARP
Parallel threads running along the length of the weave of a fabric.

WEFT
Parallel threads in the weave running along the fabric width.

WALLET CLOSURE
Cushion-cover closure formed by two overlapping pieces of fabric.

WRONG SIDES TOGETHER
Placing two pieces of fabric together back-to-back in order to sew them on the right side.

YOKE
Flat piece attached to hold a folded section.

Little tips between friends

Overlock the pieces of linen before embroidering them to avoid fraying.

Cut the pieces of linen to be embroidered on the straight grain to ensure that fabric is completely straight.

When assembling, allow a margin of at least 1-cm from the edges.

Flatten or open all of the seams with an iron.

Embroider pieces before assembling them.

Press hems with an iron, and if a mistake is made, iron the crease flat and start again.

Baste or pin before sewing.

Use 100% cotton sewing thread and not "all materials" (polyester) thread, so that the seams don't "frizz" in the wash.

For discreet seams, choose a thread colour that exactly matches the shade of the fabric or braid.

Position braids before hemming so they are well-incorporated into the seam.

Measure objects to be covered carefully before cutting the fabric and make precautionary allowances; the given dimensions are guidelines only.

Choose a ph-neutral *savon de Marseille*-based cleaning product that doesn't contain any optical brighteners, to preserve the natural colour of the linen for as long as possible.

Treat stains immediately while they are still fresh.

Avoid putting pure salt on wine stains as it fixes the tannin in the fabric; instead use white vinegar or lemon juice and rinse immediately.

Iron linen damp, pressing the iron on the linen and using slow, sweeping movements to smooth it down well.

Attach two hanging loops to tea towels, one on the short side for hanging up high, one on the long side for hanging from low furniture.

Position and baste piping with the flange towards the edge of the fabric, the part with the decorative edge pointing inwards, which later will face outwards when the work is turned right side out.

Hem towards the front of the work: the hem is then no longer hidden, but becomes a decorative element.

Reinforce seams at the corners of tea towels for more strength.

For the back of the 'message' cushions, use linen in a contrasting colour to the front.

Close the reversible pockets with the flap sometimes on one side, sometimes on the other; the fabric on the top and bottom will then be reversed.

Begin and end lengths of thread on the wrong side of the embroidery, without making a knot.

Begin a piece of embroidery by taking a 1 m length of 1 strand of Mouliné cotton, fold it in two and begin the first diagonal of the first stitch, threading the needle through the loop on the other side.

Finish your thread on the wrong side by threading it through a few existing stitches, in the same colour if possible, then cut closely.

Embroider evenweave or linen fabrics without washing them beforehand; they have been woven especially loosely for better visibility. Washing removes the fabric finish, the threads tighten up and it becomes more difficult to count them.

Embroider using one needle per thread colour; this avoids wasting time threading the same needle with each change of colour.

Go for a stroll in June in the Pays de Caux region in Normandy for the rare and secret spectacle of a field of flax in flower!

THANKS ESPECIALLY

to Sylvie Aubry, the lender of a pretty house and buyer of pretty things,
to Pascale Kogan, the maker of books unlike others.

THANKS ALSO

to Joëlle, the walking vendor and vice versa,
to Janine, the peerless sewer,
to Véronique, the astounding embroiderer,
to Françoise, the seaside embroiderer,
to Corine, the diagram-drawer of goodwill,
to Anne, the maker of pretty drawings,
to Dominique, the famous re-reader.

THANKS MOREOVER

to the embroiderers of KILA SIKU, an organisation based in Goma (Democratic Republic of Congo).
Each day in Goma, 12 women combine their efforts to ensure better living conditions for their families.
Their children are fed, cared for and go to school.

Thanks to this project, their dignity has been restored and 90 people are able to provide for themselves.
The KILA SIKU project was launched as an initiative of the Belgian non-profit organisation "En avant les enfants" in order to guarantee an income for women who, following war and the eruption of Nyiragongo Volcano in 2002, found themselves alone and without the means to raise their children.

Linen and braid used to make these projects is available from:
La Croix & la Manière
36 Rue Faidherbe
75011 Paris
33 (0)1 43 72 99 09
www.lacroixetlamanière.com

First published by Marabout in 2007
This edition published in 2009 by Murdoch Books Pty Limited

Murdoch Books Australia
Pier 8/9
23 Hickson Road
Millers Point NSW 2000
Phone: +61 (0) 2 8220 2000
Fax: +61 (0) 2 8220 2558
www.murdochbooks.com.au

Murdoch Books UK Limited
Erico House, 6th Floor
93–99 Upper Richmond Road
Putney, London SW15 2TG
Phone: +44 (0) 20 8785 5995
Fax: +44 (0) 20 8785 5985
www.murdochbooks.co.uk

Publisher: Kay Scarlett
Project Editor: Katrina O'Brien

Text, design and illustration copyright © Marabout 2007

National Library of Australia Cataloguing-in-Publication Data

Author:	Lyonnet, Monique.
Title:	Made in France Linen and thread: creating homewares embellished with embroidery and ribbon / Monique Lyonnet.
ISBN:	9781741966039 (pbk.)
Subjects:	Embroidery--Handbooks, manuals, etc.
	Embroidery--Patterns.
	Ribbon work--Handbooks, manuals, etc.
	Ribbon work--Patterns.
Dewey Number:	746.44

A catalogue record for this book is available from the British Library.

PRINTED IN CHINA. Reprinted 2011.